Surviving the Reich

The World War II Saga
of a Jewish-American GI

Ivan Goldstein

ZENITH PRESS

First published in 2010 by Zenith Press, an imprint of MBI Publishing Company, 400 First Avenue North, Suite 300, Minneapolis, MN 55401 USA

Zenith Press titles are also available at discounts in bulk quantity for industrial or sales-promotional use. For details write to Special Sales Manager at MBI Publishing Company, 400 First Avenue North, Suite 300, Minneapolis, MN 55401 USA.

To find out more about our books, visit us online at www.zenithpress.com.

ISBN-13: 978-0-7603-3816-2

LIBRARY OF CONGRESS CATALOGING-IN-PUBLICATION DATA
Goldstein, Ivan, 1924-
Surviving the Reich : the World War II saga of a
    Jewish-American GI / Ivan Goldstein.
        p. cm.
Includes bibliographical references.
ISBN 978-0-7603-3816-2 (hbk. w/jkt)
1. Goldstein, Ivan, 1924- 2. World War, 1939-1945–Personal narratives, Jewish. 3. World War, 1939-1945–Personal narratives, American. 4. World War, 1939-1945–Participation, Jewish. 5. Stalag XII A. 6. World War, 1939-1945–Prisoners and prisons, German. 7. Jewish soldiers–United States–Biography. 8. Jewish veterans–United States–Biography. 9. Goldstein, Ivan, 1924–Family. I. Title.
    D811.G617 2010
    940.54'7243092--dc22
    [B]
                    2009036827

Designer: Diana Boger
Design Manager: Brenda C. Canales
Cover Design: Rob Johnson

CREDITS
On the cover: The gate of Stalag XII A guarded by Allied troops after the liberation. *Allan Jackson/Keystone/Getty Images*

On the back cover: M4 Sherman tanks in the snow during the Battle of the Bulge. *Department of Defense*

Printed in the United States of America

*In Honor of June,
my wife and helpmate for sixty wonderful years
of support, encouragement, and inspiration.*

In Memory of my Mother and Father.

Contents

Preface

WRITING A BOOK ABOUT MY LIFE at the age of eighty-three is like watching a movie through a dreamlike haze. Some recollections stand out in vivid detail; others flit by, barely there at all. A major part of this memoir is made up of my World War II experiences, a period of only two and a half years, but how I reacted to that episode has everything to do with my earlier years, and its impact has resonated throughout my life, even when I was least aware of it.

So this is a book of discovery, in a way. More than just a narrative of challenging encounters, it is a work that I hope will offer its readers—among them, my own descendants—a demonstration of the strength of our human spirit and the resilience of faith.

Though sometimes treated as a hero, I did not feel like one at the time. I was a simple soldier, charged at the age of nineteen with the formidable task of eradicating evil from the world. At least, that is how we viewed our mission—my army pals and I. Over these many years, I have acquired a meaningful perspective of that era, and I have gained insights worth sharing.

You could say that at eighty-three, I've learned a thing or two.

—Ivan Goldstein, Jerusalem, 2008

Acknowledgments

FIRST OF ALL, I would like to thank my wonderful editor Charlotte Friedland for her expertise and advice and for guiding me through unfamiliar territory.

Thanks to my son Daniel, who for many years has constantly insisted that this story be told. Also thanks to my son David, whose valuable assistance helped in the completion of the final draft of the book. Thanks to my granddaughter, Nechama, for the countless hours she spent typing the manuscript. Thanks to my friend Martin Zerobnick for his honesty and knowledge in the proof-reading of the book.

I owe a special debt of gratitude to my three army buddies, Jules Levine, Ted Hartman, and Wayne Van Dyke, as well as to Greg Urda and Bob Anderson, who never stopped pushing me to write the book. Thanks to my friend Roger Marquet, without whose dogged determination in finding the *Barracuda* this story would never have been told.

I owe the greatest thanks to the two main women in my life: my mother, of blessed memory, who is one of the main characters of the book and was the guiding and primary influence of my life, and my wife, June, for her input and wise counsel on every phase of the story. But mostly I wish to thank June for her love, guidance, and companionship over the past sixty years. She is my life.

CHAPTER 1

Early Years

IT WAS A SUNDAY, a warm, beautiful, December day in Denver. The year was 1941, and I was seventeen years old. My mother had given me a number of chores to do, and I was now on the last of the list —"Beat rugs."

I lined up four rugs on the clothesline in our back yard and started taking some mighty and rapid swings with my Louisville Slugger. As the rolls of dust rose in the clear Colorado air, I became transformed into baseball star Ted Williams, lifting a monumental shot into the centerfield bleachers.

It's the World Series, bottom of the ninth, two out, one run behind, one runner on base. I am up at the plate, ready for the pitch. I hear the sportscaster shout, "It's a fastball down the middle!" I watch the ball and . . . wham! The ball flies long, high, and out of sight.

The scream "Ivan!" shattered my imaginary moment. Mother's voice was frantic. I ran through the back door and up a few steps into the kitchen. The breakfast nook had a long, narrow table with a built-in bench on either side. At the end of the table under the window was a mahogany Irvin table radio.

Mother was sitting next to the radio, her expression frozen with alarm. The reporter was blurting, "Japanese airplanes have attacked Pearl Harbor . . . great damage . . . many casualties. . . ." My brother and I sat with Mother in the breakfast nook. We leaned in toward the radio, listening to the sketchy news, as the reporter tried desperately to sound calm.

I had promised my friends earlier that I would join their football game, and I raced my bike to the park, my mind in turmoil. My friends had not heard about Pearl Harbor, and the weight of the shocking news overshadowed the game. Would there be war? Should we enlist in the army? The football in my hands seemed childish now, as if I somehow understood that my boyhood would soon be over.

At ten o'clock the next morning, our principal, Mr. Hill, assembled the entire faculty and student body of East Denver High in the auditorium. A stern disciplinarian, old Hill looked more somber than ever before. The stage was empty except for a large console radio. There was an unnatural silence as the familiar voice of the president of the United States, Franklin Delano Roosevelt, filled the room.

Packed together in that auditorium, we heard our president declare, "Yesterday, December 7, 1941—a date which will live in infamy—the United States was suddenly and deliberately attacked by naval and air forces of the Empire of Japan. . . . Yesterday the Japanese government also launched an attack against Malaya . . . Hong Kong . . . Guam . . . the Philippine Islands . . . [and] Midway Island . . . I assert that we will not only defend ourselves to the uttermost, but will make it very certain that this form of treachery shall never endanger us again."

We were at war! That day, all we could talk about was how our lives and our country had changed overnight, and how both would never again be the same. World War II, which had seemed so far away, hit home.

Until now, no threat had loomed so large on my mental landscape. Though I had grown up during the Great Depression, I was not rushed into adulthood too quickly as others my age had been. My childhood had been a joyous time, despite the fact that my father died when I was very young. This normalcy and contented lifestyle was entirely the work of my mother. But we are getting ahead of ourselves.

Some of my earliest childhood memories are the times that I spent at my grandparents' house in Denver. These memories are mostly associated with the Jewish holidays and Shabbos (Sabbath). From the age of three to five and a half years old, I remember my brother Jerry and me walking on Shabbos with my mother to my grandparents. There was always a delicious Shabbos lunch. I still remember Bubbie's (Grandmother's) homemade gefilte fish and *chrain* (horseradish sauce). She had the reputation as the best cook in the family. I remember my grandfather with his beautiful voice singing Shabbos *zmiros* (songs) during lunch. Later, Zaidy (Grandfather) would cuddle with us in his bed with a large feather comforter and tell us wonderful stories from the Bible and stories about his youth. Finally, I would drift into sleep after hearing the tales that left such a deep impression on me.

My grandmother Taube Esther Greinetz died about a week before Passover. I was five and a half years old at the time. One of the most vivid memories that left its imprint on my youth occurred at the night of the Passover Seder. The entire family of aunts, uncles, and cousins was assembled at my zaidy's Seder table. The family had just finished the shiva, the week-long period of mourning following the death of a close relative in the Jewish tradition. As one of the youngest grandchildren, I was sitting next to my zaidy and listened as he read and sang the Haggadah. I remember the tears rolling down his cheeks the entire night, some even landing on me. I remember his beautiful booming voice being interrupted by his crying and choking.

A few weeks before my bubbie's death, my Brooklyn zaidy (my father's father) had died, seven months after I had met and visited with the Goldstein family in

4

Max and Ida Goldstein, 1920. To hear Mother tell it, theirs was the greatest love of the century. She never remarried.

Father and Mother worked side by side in their first store.
Photos taken around 1923 show the beautiful shop, with
Mother behind the counter.

Brooklyn. Despite losing two grandparents, at the age
of five I was too young to understand the implications
or meaning of death. However, only six months later the
sudden and untimely death of my father would change
the circumstances and direction of my young life.

A simple tooth extraction led to an infection that took
him from us quickly and without warning. My brother
Jerry was eight years old, I was almost six, and Mother, in
her thirties, was in the first month of another pregnancy.
As though it were yesterday, I can still hear her piercing
screams of anguish, yelling with despair, as I came home
from school on that fateful day. My cousin Howard met
me outside. "Don't go in there, Ivan," he warned. "You
don't want to go in just now."

I stayed outdoors for what seemed like hours, listening to Mother's cries punctuated by the deep, soothing voices of her family. I wanted to run to Mother, hug her, and tell her that everything would be all right, but I was afraid to go near the house where terrible things were going on.

They said I wouldn't understand. Deemed too young to attend the funeral, Jerry and I were kept at home while the grownups went about their grim, mysterious business.

Though Father's death didn't seem quite real to me, Mother's inconsolable grief now hung like a thick black veil over our home. Where there had once been laughter and song, there was mourning and worry. What would become of us?

Because of Mother's initial state of shock and grief, her sister Libby and Uncle Joe, who were wealthy, convinced

The original Murph's logo was designed by my father, Max "Murph" Goldstein. Murph was the nickname given to my father while growing up on the Lower East Side of New York.

her to move temporarily into their large home for the shiva period and until she could regain her bearings and plan for her future. Every morning, Uncle Joe's chauffeur would drive us in his limousine to Teller Elementary School. Even at that young age, I was a little embarrassed by this ostentation, especially since our fancy arrival belied the fact that we were, in truth, penniless.

But Mother had no intention of staying long in their home. She would pull herself together; she would manage on her own. She would raise the children and provide for them, Depression or no Depression. Regardless of what others may have thought, Mother was not one to languish in self-pity. She had a job to do. It was clear to her that she must be mother, father, breadwinner, and teacher to her lively, growing family.

Only a month after the shiva, Mother had already taken steps toward financial independence and moved us out of her sister's home. Our father had owned a jewelry and gift store, but it had gone into bankruptcy along with millions of other businesses during the Great Depression. The fixtures and merchandise from the shop were in storage with the bankruptcy court. Somehow, Mother convinced the court to release everything to her. Perhaps she was entitled to it, or perhaps the court took pity on this recently widowed young woman, soon expecting her fatherless child, who so resolutely had decided to stand on her own. In either case, the goods were signed over to her.

Against the odds, Mother reopened Murph's. This photo of
318 Seventeenth Street, where Murph's was in business for over
thirty-five years, was taken shortly before Murph's was moved to
its final location.

For Fine Jewelry and Watch Repairing

SEE

Murph's Jewelry & Gift Shop
OPPOSITE BROWN PALACE HOTEL
ALL WORK GUARANTEED

Gifts and Souvenirs
Indian Jewelry
Colorado Alabaster

318 SEVENTEENTH STREET
DENVER, COLORADO

9

At the train station in Denver in 1924, the year I was born, my zaidy, bubbie, and their youngest daughter, Mashie (Margaret), set off on the first leg of their trip to Palestine for Mashie's wedding in Jerusalem. It was my grandparents' first visit and would set in motion their plans to move to Palestine. Five and a half years later my grandmother died, and Zaidy moved to Palestine in 1931.

Zaidy's grocery store.

Next, she needed a place to set up shop. Padding up and down the streets of downtown Denver, she hoped against all reason to find an empty store for which the landlord would not demand the usual down payment for a month-to-month lease. At last, she found one. It was a perfect location, too, for it was across the street from the Brown Palace Hotel, a famous landmark erected in the late 1800s. Murph's Jewelry and Gift Shop was once again open for business!

My grandfather had sold his house and moved into Aunt Libby's home, already having made the decision to realize his lifelong dream to live in Palestine. All of his children adamantly disagreed with his wishes, except for

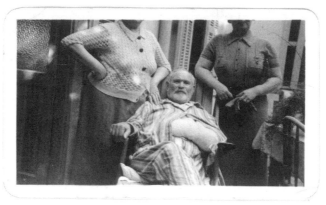

Zaidy just before his death in 1938.

my mother, who was closer to him and needed him the most. She supported him 100 percent, and she knew that his ultimate wish must be carried out.

The memory of the entire family bidding Zaidy Greinetz goodbye at the railroad station still remains a vivid memory. This was the last time we would see Zaidy, although I remember mother reading us his letters through the years. He settled in Tel Aviv, and eight years later we would hear of his death.

Throughout the years growing up in Denver, numerous times I would make contact with older people who said they knew my grandparents, Abraham and Taube Esther Greinetz. These conversations were in glowing, thankful terms:

"When I came to Denver from Europe, it was your grandfather who got me my first job."

"He was instrumental in starting me out in business."

"It was your grandparents who made our wedding."

"It was your grandmother who supplied the layette and took part in the delivery of my first child."

"Your grandfather supplied us with groceries when we couldn't afford them."

"Your grandmother was a true *tzadikkas*; no one knows of the many families that she helped."

"If it was not for your grandparents, our families never could have made it."

These encounters proved the saying, "A good name is more precious than rubies."

My little brother was born on July 3, 1931, while I was sick with the measles. He was named Max, after my father. Whenever he was called by his Hebrew name in the synagogue or shul, "Mordechai ben [son of] Mordechai," strangers would lift their eyebrows and stare with pity, for our custom is to name babies only after deceased relations. "How did this poor child wind up with his own father's name?" they'd wonder. But the people in our shul, our family, our friends, and our neighbors knew.

Mother's resourcefulness met the challenge of caring for her newborn while running a full-time business. Because of the Depression, farm girls were readily available as maids and babysitters. Mother offered three dollars per week, with room and board, for a live-in sitter. And she found a gem—Julia Sturdavant came to live with us

Mother was an avid reader, well versed in Shakespeare, the classics, and contemporary works, and she easily transmitted her love of reading. One of our favorite bedtime rituals was that she would read a chapter or two of a library book to us. A favorite book was *Mrs. Wiggs of the Cabbage Patch*, by Alice C. H. Rice, about a widowed mother who struggled to support her children. Mrs. Wiggs, with her plucky spirit and unshakable determination, mirrored our own mother, subtly comforting and inspiring us. Clockwise from top: Ivan, Mother, Max, and Jerome.

and remained for three years. Julia made Mother's work possible, though not easy.

Mother's family tried to convince her to remarry and to put the children in the Home for Jewish Children in Denver. "No," she replied ardently to their pleas. She would not remarry. And true to her word, she remained alone.

At least, I thought she was alone, until one day she confided to us that she had taken on a "business partner." When the lights suddenly had gone out of her sparkling life, when all seemed bleak and the dread of poverty had gripped her, she cried out, "Dear God! Give me the strength to raise these children, to bring food to our table. Please help me, and I promise You that I will give all I possibly can to charity!" It was a pledge she kept all her life, and her Partner never let her down. We were not rich, but we always had enough to eat.

Every morning, Mother would get up at five thirty, prepare our breakfast, lunches, and evening dinner, and send Jerry and me off to school. She would nurse Maxie and then take the streetcar downtown to work. In late morning, she would lock up the store, take the streetcar home, nurse the baby again, and go back to work. Day in and day out, she continued this taxing routine. If she ever was sick, we never knew about it. She seemed indestructible.

Of course, she needed help in the store but couldn't afford it. As each of us grew big enough to stand behind the counter, Mother trained us to be competent and reliable workers. We were proud to be able to help her, and the skills she taught us were invaluable: good salesmanship, making change, wrapping packages, measuring a proper ring size. The vast knowledge we acquired specific to jewelry has stayed with me all my life. We learned about precious and semiprecious gemstones, as well as copper, gold, silver, and platinum. We knew how to buy, test, and weigh old gold that customers wanted to sell; to understand the intricacies of all types of jewelry; and how to change watch crystals and bands. Moreover, a large part of our stock was hand-made silver and turquoise jewelry, pottery, beaded items, and woven materials from the Indians in the region. We became little experts in the symbols and histories of different Indian tribes.

As Mother's errand boys, we had the responsibility of taking expensive jewelry to repair shops and wholesale establishments. And we all pitched in to keep the front windows, display cases, and cabinets sparkling.

The best part of working in the store was meeting unusual people. Whether tourists or Denverites, we were fascinated by them. With the diverse and eclectic knowledge of a prolific reader, Mother attracted a broad assortment of "regulars" to Murph's. There was the peanut man, who sold small bags of roasted peanuts from his worn, brown leather suitcase. His expertise was politics, and he often lectured us on the world's political situation. He felt so strongly about the Spanish Civil War that he went off to Spain to fight against Nationalist Gen. Francisco Franco, and for years afterward, he talked incessantly about his experiences there. Then there was Chief Hawkins, a Sioux Indian chief, who brought his homemade items to sell at our store. For hours, he and Mother would exchange information about Indian and Jewish histories and cultures. "I tell you, Ivan," he would say, winking conspiratorially, "the Sioux must be one of the Lost Tribes of Israel. We're so much alike!"

"The Pickle Man" was always dressed in an old, tattered suit and a stained tie. Aged, but in robust health, he attributed his longevity to eating a dill pickle every day. His expertise was in antiques and fine art. He spent many hours a week in the public library researching this passion. The highlight of his life was securing a folder of original Daumier etchings.

These are only a few of the many people whom my mother befriended. Inadvertently, she was teaching me one of the most valuable of lessons: never judge people by their dress or status in life. I learned to respect everyone, to feel empathy for every human being, to value the knowledge of others, and to respect their interests. It is only by being a living example of this ethic that you can teach others. Many people espouse these values; Mother lived them.

She was our religious mentor, too. She had been born and raised in the religious Jewish community of Denver, and she persistently tried to pass on this precious heritage to us. It was not always easy to do this, for some assimilated members of our family derided religion and chided her for being old-fashioned. She stood up for Judaism as a way of life, keeping a kosher home and infusing our Sabbath with as much warmth and beauty as she could.

Though not strictly observant (for she felt compelled to work on Saturdays), Mother made it a point to keep us surrounded by role models with clear Jewish convictions and practices. As we grew older, we considered it a privilege to prepare for Shabbos, and we all had chores to do. (My job was washing the floors, and I became quite an expert at it.) On Friday night, she would recite Kiddush, the prayer sanctifying this holy time, and then she'd serve one of her wonderful Shabbos meals. Who could refuse a second helping of stuffed *helzel* (chicken neck) with its rich, smooth dressing, or chicken soup with eggs and lima bean crisps?

On Friday nights, we sang in the synagogue choir, an experience that enriched us in numerous ways for the rest of our lives. "You have good, strong voices like your father's," Mother would tell us, though we knew that her voice, too, was sweet and melodious. Singing with us at bedtime, she taught us dozens upon dozens of songs— snatches of everything from Eastern European lullabies to American folk songs to popular Broadway hits.

Mom sent us to *cheder*, an afternoon Hebrew school that taught us the basics of reading Hebrew and prayers. Jerry would play hooky from *cheder* now and then, and you could be sure that our cousin Morton would report Jerry's absence to his mother. She, in turn, would call our Mom, beginning the conversation with, "Did you know your son

Great Uncle Israel Block had a profound influence on me. He is shown here on the porch swing of his home at 1854 Hooker Street.

wasn't in *cheder* today?" And Mother would take it from there, resorting to the tried-and-true method of spanking her errant son. Though I too would rather have been playing ball, I didn't really mind Hebrew school. Some of the teachers were European, and they gave us a peek into the world they had come from—a world known to my great-grandparents, rich in folklore and sturdy in its beliefs.

My great uncle, Israel Block, was married to my grandmother's sister, Aunt Leah. Uncle Block (as we called him) was a Rabbi who taught at the *cheder* on the west side of Denver (the more religious area of Denver). They were childless. After my grandmother died and Zaidy left for Palestine, Uncle Block and Aunt Leah filled the role

Left to right: Ivan, Maxie, and Jerry.

of grandparents for the three Goldstein boys growing up in Denver. We spent the Passover Seders at their home and ate festive meals in their *sukkah* (temporary dwelling) during the holiday of Sukkoth. Mother sent us to stay at the Blocks' at every opportunity to supply us with a religious experience and feeling that was missing on the east side of Denver, and we absorbed some of Uncle Block's intangible and firm commitment to Judaism.

But the solid core of ideals came from Mother. With wisdom inherited from her forefathers and mothers, she knew that the way to bind a child to enduring faith was to teach it at home—not preach, mind you. Mother didn't lecture. She would take us for tours of her birthplace and the old neighborhood, the west side of Denver that was rich in shuls. It even had a *shvitz,* a steam bath that was nearly sacred territory to three generations. (Today, the Denver Broncos football team plays in the stadium built on that site. Could it be that some places are forever destined for sweat?) She would punctuate these visits with true stories—some funny, others poignant—colorful tales of what it was like to grow up at the turn of the century among workers and tradesmen, midwives and merchants, neighbors who were like family. She even told us about the *chevra kaddisha,* the burial society, where volunteers tenderly prepared the dead for burial, and how the entire community would mourn every family's loss as their own. At bedtime, she would regale us with more stories—about her grandmother arriving in Denver in a covered wagon

21

even before Colorado became a state; and about her father's horse, Jack, who seemed to sense on Friday afternoons that soon it would be Shabbos and would gallop home extra fast. And she taught by example about what it means to be kind and caring; to share all you have with others; to trust in God to see you through the tough times.

Despite the hard facts of her struggle, she had us convinced that life is fun, taking us to summer band concerts, museums, and shows. She laughed with us and allowed us the freedom to explore our world. She saw beauty in everything, and so did we.

I had no idea how great her challenges were until an eye-opening incident occurred in my early teens. One summer evening, Jerry and I had been watching the semi-pro softball games at City Park. After the games, we decided to play ball with friends in the park. Mother would come home quite late from the store in the summers (for the tourist trade made it worth her while), and she naturally expected us to be home when she got there. But we lost track of time and got home after midnight. Mother was frantic. She had searched for her missing boys and called everyone we knew.

When we walked in the door, all of her fears and anxieties poured out in a harangue so loud that it woke my uncle and aunt, who lived next door. I will never forget Uncle Harvey leaning out of his window and shouting, "Ida, stop yelling! We told you to put the kids in a home! You can't raise them yourself!"

We all froze, immobilized by his impetuous revelation. "Just go to bed," Mom muttered to us, her head drooping. Till then, I had never known that after Father's death she had stood up to intense family pressure to remarry and put us in an orphanage, a commonplace practice at the time. I hadn't realized how desperate she was to raise us well, all by herself. Now it was all clear, and the sharpness of that moment cut through me, never to be forgotten.

But when President Roosevelt declared war, my first thought was of what I owed my country, not my family. Like many of my friends, I wanted to enlist in the army, but Mother said no. She had lost her husband early in life, and she had no intention of risking her son.

No was no.

Instead, she urged me to enroll in college after my high school graduation in June 1942. As far as she was concerned, I could sit out the war in a classroom. I didn't argue. The University of Denver admitted me as an art major, and I was truly glad to be able to develop my interests and talent. As most of the fellows had gone off to war, I was one of the few males on campus. Surrounded by girls in every class, I reasoned that maybe staying in school wasn't so bad after all.

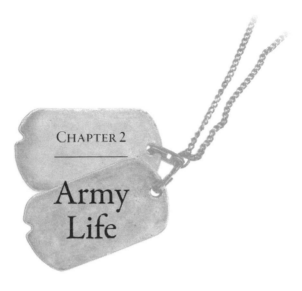

CHAPTER 2

Army Life

A S THE WAR PRESSED ON, rationing became a way of life; conservation of useful materials was our national duty. Like all other Americans, the Goldsteins pitched in to the war effort. Ours has been called "The Greatest Generation," for we had slogged through the Great Depression and readily took on whatever challenges faced us. We had been toughened and grown practical: we were accustomed to do without. So what if we had to limit meat, sugar, butter? You want fresh vegetables? Grow them in your victory garden! Like twenty million other Americans, we seeded and weeded and watered our backyard. And we managed.

Citizens participated in conservation measures with deadly earnest. Because of food shortages, families were issued food-rationing stamps to be used at their grocery stores, redeeming them twice a week, on Tuesdays and Thursdays. Because cooking fat renderings could be used in the production of certain munitions, the public was asked to save their cooking fat wastes. Collection stations were in neighborhood grocery stores, and the grocers would collect and turn in the cans of fat. Because of the demands of this system, manpower at the stores would sometimes be unable to keep up with the volume of donations. One day I was passing by Miller's, a local grocery chain store, when I noticed a sign posted on the front window. I always regretted not taking a photo of this sign, as it easily could have taken top prize in a competition. It read, "Ladies, please do not bring in your fat cans on Tuesdays or Thursdays, as our clerks cannot handle them."

Everyone listened intently to the radio and scanned the newspapers for an encouraging word from the front, soberly accepting the idea that winning the war was vital to the United States, to Europe, to all humanity. Never since has the vast majority of our population been fully supportive of a war.

My draft notice came in the winter of 1942, but the army allowed me to postpone my induction until the end of the spring quarter. Today, patriotism is considered naïve. But back then, if your country called you, you went. Mother was beside herself. Though proud that I qualified for service, her heart was torn in two. We all knew that Hitler was

My original dog tags.

perpetrating some kind of genocide on our people. We had heard horrible stories—stories that just couldn't possibly be true—yet we didn't dare ignore them. Most Americans, and certainly every Jew, felt that this evil must be defeated at all costs. But to send her Ivan into the fray?

There was no choice, of course. It was July 1943, the day before my induction. I went swimming with some friends and fell asleep poolside for hours in the sizzling Colorado sun. The sunburn was unimaginably painful. Looking back on it, I probably should have gone to a hospital, but we were accustomed to taking care of ourselves, and I was determined not to be delayed in going into the service the next day with my friends. Mother treated the burn all night long with her usual expertise and tenderness.

Scalded red, with my skin stinging at the slightest touch, I reported for duty at Fort Logan Army Induction Center on the outskirts of Denver. During the next few days, we were fitted for uniforms, took IQ tests, got our GI haircuts, and attended classes and briefings. Superiors urged me to report to the infirmary to treat the sunburn, but I refused. I was given a two-day pass to say goodbye to my family, and when I returned to Fort Logan we received orders to ship out.

I was now on a troop train bound for sunny and glamorous California. We were going to Camp Roberts, a huge newly constructed center for infantry and field artillery training located midway between Los Angeles and San Francisco. Did I particularly want artillery training? No, but unlike enlisted men, draftees were given no choices. The basic training was with 155mm howitzers (large, field artillery cannons) and the program was intense. We were put through grueling physical training designed to shape untrained, out-of-condition men into battle-ready soldiers. Completely occupied by day, at night I would fall into my bunk, totally exhausted. But on Sunday, our day off, homesickness would overtake me, and I would call home to talk to Mother.

I remained there only until November; my career in the field artillery was ended by the creative kindness of the Jewish army chaplain. I had been attending Friday night services as regularly as possible, for my boyhood choir experience had grown into a love of the familiar liturgy and

Private Ivan L. Goldstein.

a longing for Jewish connections. Besides, we were given kosher salami sandwiches—an extra taste of home. The chaplain took a fatherly interest in the nineteen-year-old from Denver who loved to sing and was kind enough to recommend me for the Army Specialized Training Program (ASTP): eighteen months of college courses in languages, engineering, and meteorology. A few days before we were to receive our orders to ship out to the Pacific theater, orders came through for me to take the ASTP admissions test at Compton Junior College in Los Angeles. Somehow, I passed the entrance exams in engineering, and they sent me to the University of Oregon in Eugene.

In the Army Specialized Training Program (ASTP) at the University of Oregon, 1943. Our country was at war, and it was only a matter of time before I would be sent overseas.

This was nothing like army life—living in a beautiful dormitory room, on a gorgeous campus, eating special food. Compared to the army, it was like living in a country club. My roommate was a bright young man from Connecticut named Richard Grossman. Prior to induction, he had started college with plans to become a doctor and had taken most of the science courses that we were taking in the first semester at ASTP. This was merely review for him. We had been warned that students who did not pass with high grades would not be kept in the program, and he offered his help in tutoring, which I gratefully accepted. After the first three months,

I passed the tests with good grades and was guaranteed the next three-month program. We were to receive a short furlough home before the new session started. Then came a sudden announcement that landed like a bombshell.

The army was planning a major invasion in Europe, and military experts anticipated that the losses in human life would be heavy. ASTP was a luxury the army could no longer afford: It needed fighters, not college boys. The entire program was shut down in universities nationwide, and my pals and I—all engineering students—were sent to Camp Cooke, California, where a battle-ready division awaited us.

We arrived by train on a Sunday, and I was assigned to Company B, 41st Tank Battalion, along with three other students: Jules Levine, Ted Hartman, and Wayne Van Dyke. A warm and close friendship between our foursome was to develop during our service. (Some fifty-five years later, an incredible event was to occur that would reunite the four of us.)

Our first day of duty with Company B wouldn't start until the next day, so I decided to go to the movie at the post theater. While standing in the ticket line, someone struck the back of my knees, almost knocking me to the ground. I swung around, arms up, ready to protect myself—only to see, with great surprise, my cousin Howard Greinetz, who had just arrived with his ASTP unit. Howard told me that in the last letter he received from Denver, his father wrote that our great-uncle Israel Block had died. The *cheder rebbe,* the loving uncle whose warm Jewish influence had enfolded me as a child and strengthened me as a young adult, would not be there for me anymore. I felt like an orphan once again.

There was no time to grieve, however, for the next morning, we were assembled to be briefed by our company commander, the captain who would become my unrelenting foe and nemesis for the next eight and a half months—you could say, the bane of my army existence. The confrontations between the two of us were bitter and constant. My resolve was that he would not break me and I would become a good soldier despite his dislike toward me.

We were hustled into a crash course in mastering the Sherman tank. We college kids were trained as bow gunners—the lowest job of the five positions in the tank, for we had the least training. For five months, we were schooled in the operation of this workhorse of a weapon. It was lighter than the German tanks, we were told, and could move faster. The bad news was that the thin armor surrounding us would never stand up to the powerful, piercing shells of the German tanks. So the name of the game was to outmaneuver the German tanks, disabling them before they could get a good shot at us. That was the theory.

But before I would face the enemy, I had to deal with my more immediate problem. I surmised that the captain's disdain for me was rooted deeper than a common resentment of raw recruits. I had seen that look before. In

Denver, as in many other places, the local Catholic school taught that Jews were Christkillers, tacitly encouraging their students to bully Jewish children. They would walk around the neighborhood in groups and look for Jewish kids walking alone to challenge or attack. If one of these gangs found you, you had better be able to handle yourself. A Jew learned to run, fight, and judge which one was better at any given moment. In short, I had to learn to size up a situation quickly and to take care of myself, and the lesson turned out to be a critical one later in my life.

But I was unprepared for such an attitude from my tank commander. Maybe it was the fact that, unlike others on the base, I didn't hide my Jewish background and, in fact, was proud of it. Maybe it had nothing to do with the fact that I was Jewish, but more because I wasn't afraid of him, or of anybody else, for that matter. Whatever the reason, the captain's antipathy for me was unmistakable.

One of our early confrontations was just before Passover. It was a time of the year that I sorely missed being home. Every year, before Pesach, Mother would mobilize our whole family to clean the entire house. Cabinets, floors, walls, mattresses—everything was scrubbed down until our home was scented with a special pre-Pesach freshness. We'd all pitch in, straining and sweating, until Mom was satisfied. Then the work of bringing up the special dishes from the basement would begin. Within a day or two, the house would again smell different: this time with the heavenly cooking aromas of special Passover foods.

So I was thrilled when Mother sent me a box of matzoh; it was a practical measure, for Mother knew I wouldn't eat bread, which is forbidden on Passover. But more than that, it was a touch of home, and it brought back the warmth of her magical kitchen. I put the box in my footlocker, which was against the rules, for we were not allowed to keep food there. It was unopened, and I intended to take it to the mess hall to store for me during the eight days of Passover.

That day, when I came back from maneuvers, I found that the whole box of matzoh had been opened, broken up, and dumped all over my bed. I was told to report to the captain's office.

"Captain, I found the box of matzoh that my mother sent me destroyed, and the contents were dumped on my bed. I was told to report to you."

"That's right. You knew that it was against regulations to store food in your footlocker."

"But that was my food for Passover! My mother sent it because I can't eat bread next week."

"That's your problem. You broke the rules."

"Couldn't you have just confiscated it? Couldn't you have put it somewhere else, instead of breaking it all?"

"That's it, private! You've got KP duty next week. Dismissed!" KP meant kitchen police, referring to soldiers assigned to help in the kitchen. As peeling potatoes and hauling tons of garbage is not exactly an elite job, KP duty was commonly used as a punishment.

In our barracks, Friday night was the time to scrub the place clean. When I asked for permission to go to my chapel services, the captain refused my request, implying that I was pulling the religion card to get out of the cleaning. I offered to make up the work, but he still refused to let me go.

According to regulations, Christians were off on Sunday so they could attend church, and Jews were permitted to go to Friday night services. Going to these services was the only Jewish experience open to me in the army, and since boyhood, I had loved going to shul. I knew that it was my right to go to the services of my faith, so I went to the major, the battalion commander. Again, I offered to give up passes, to take on extra work. The major was startled and puzzled by my desperate entreaties. "You have the right to worship," he said gently, "without having to offer anything in return. Your commanding officer must know that. Here," he said, signing a paper, "take this order to your captain."

The captain was furious! From then on, he gave me extra guard duty and found fault with everything I did. He was trying to break me, trying to get me to give up Friday night services—but that was my little bit of Shabbos, and I wasn't going to let anyone take it from me.

Yes, we Jews had our rights at Camp Cooke, but that didn't eradicate the sentiments around us. On one particular occasion, the entire camp was gathered for an update on current events when a soldier stood up and asked, "Why are we going into battle, risking our lives, while the Jews make money off this war?" He was allowed to continue, piling on more anti-Semitic statements, totally unchallenged. The blithe answer was, "That's not for us to say; we have a job to do."

There was no negation of the "facts" implied in the question, no denial, nor censure of the soldier's attitude. I was burning.

Outside, after the session, I took a long look at the questioner. He was a surly guy and looked tough, but I decided to confront him anyway. I gave him a piece of my mind, and fists flew. The captain came out and saw the scuffle, broke it up, and noted the bloody nose I had given the other guy. The "victim" got a sympathetic pat on the back and went free. For me: more KP.

After everyone had left, a soldier came up to me and whispered, "For what it's worth, I feel for you because I'm Jewish too," adding hastily, "but nobody knows it." I realized he had been able to hide his identity because his last name sounded Italian.

"Why do you hide it?" I challenged him.

"It's better for me this way," he answered furtively. "It's just better."

I surmise that there were many such "Marranos" in the military in those days. Ethnic pride had not yet evolved in the melting pot that was America in the 1940s. Being a Jew bore a stigma in many circles, and most people just wanted to blend in. At best, your Star of David was worn under your shirt, or simply carried in your heart.

There's another little postscript to this story. When we arrived in France, the "tough guy" shot himself in the leg (he said, "by accident") and he never did have to go into battle.

Even normal, fair treatment for Private Goldstein was beyond my favorite officer's ken, and he discriminated in many unanticipated ways. Take the target competition, for instance. Back in 1944—before computers!—to aim a tank's gun, you had to estimate distance visually and then adjust the sight. Tank training included target practice, and for some reason, we ASTP guys excelled at this. Accuracy testing included everyone, including tank commanders, and the object was to see how many shells it took you to hit the target. To motivate the men, prizes were offered, and test results were posted on the bulletin board for all to see. And what prize did a soldier want most? A three-day pass!

How excited I was when I saw that I had scored the highest, even surpassing the officers. I promptly strode over to the captain's office to collect my prize. "No pass!" he hissed, and threw me out with a barrage of nasty names.

I didn't go over his head this time. I figured he was baiting me so I would do something wrong: then he could have me court-martialed. I didn't play his little game. I sure could have used the pass, though. During all the months of training, he had denied me all requests for furlough.

But when I got my orders to go overseas, I knew I was entitled to a furlough for a visit home. I really wanted that furlough. I knew my mother would be waiting to see me before I left, that she would treasure our time together. I wanted to be able to tell her I loved her, that I'd be ok, that I'd be back. But even now, the captain said no, no furlough. My blood boiled. He had no right to keep me from seeing my family before going into battle! I knew the army regulations, and I went over his head to get my rightful pass. I didn't care if later I would have to pay for his displeasure. I went back to Denver to say goodbye.

As it happened, I returned the week of Max's Bar Mitzvah. I requested an extended leave so I could stay for Shabbos and celebrate with my family. Request denied. Resigned to the dictates of war, the whole family accompanied me to the train station to say goodbye. I hugged each one and kissed Mother, assuring her that I would be back soon. She gave me a long, sorrowful look.

Since I could not stay for Max's Bar Mitzvah, I did the next best thing: I wrote a letter to Max, loaded with sage advice from a big brother. Many years later, when we were both grown and had children and grandchildren of our own, I discovered that Max had cherished that letter his whole life.

CHAPTER 3

Going Overseas

MY DIVISION WAS DECLARED COMBAT READY, and our days in the States were drawing to a close. Most of the men had been training for close to two years. At the time that the division had been formed, in August 1942, General Rommel was threatening the Suez Canal, Cairo, and the Allied supply line in the Middle East. The new division was formed to meet the challenge, and it would signal the increasing role of armor in the Army's upcoming campaigns. Thousands of young recruits had been sent to Camp Polk, Louisiana, for the rigorous and tireless training. After eight months the 11th Armored Division was sent to Camp Barkley, Texas, for yet more training and then to the Mojave Desert of California, where desert battle conditions were simulated. From there, they were transferred to Camp Cooke for organizational training and to polish their battle skills.

Unlike the well-trained core of the division, the ASTP soldiers, myself included, had been rushed through just five months of training. But that didn't matter. The war needed men, hundreds of thousands of men, to meet a vicious and seemingly unstoppable enemy. Ironically, despite its desert training, the 11th Armored was slated to take part in a huge campaign in Western Europe.

On August 12, 1944, we received orders to go to Camp Kilmer in New Jersey, our point of embarkation. My Division left Camp Cooke in September. To confuse the enemy, the battalion was divided into two groups taking different railroad routes through the country. Our company traveled through the South. The first morning, we got out of the train in Arizona for calisthenics, and I enjoyed an unexpected pleasure: the sun was rising over the Painted Desert, and it was a beautiful sight to behold. We traveled through New Mexico and Texas during an intense heat wave. At each train stop, the townspeople would be waiting with ice-cold lemonade and other treats for us. The wonderful unity and warmth that they felt toward their servicemen was exhibited everywhere across America. I doubt that we will ever again experience such unanimity in our country. The trip took six days and nights, and we finally arrived at Camp Kilmer.

We received M4 Sherman training in California's Mojave Desert but would end up serving in wintery Western Europe. *Official U.S. Army Photo*

Orders were issued that every division member should have the opportunity to visit New York City. My father's family lived in Brooklyn, and I realized that I would have time to pay them a visit before shipping out.

I had been to New York as a very young child, when Father had gone east with Jerry and me to see his family. It had taken two days to get there by train, and we stayed a month. I was overwhelmed by the swirl of grandparents, uncles, aunts, and cousins who seemed to know all about me, though I had never met them before. Zaidy Goldstein had been the biggest surprise of all. A small man with round glasses, he had come from Russia after a stay in Ireland. And he looked like an Irishman too, with blond hair and blues eyes, which my father inherited. Though my father's given name was Max, he was nicknamed Murph growing up on the Lower East Side of New York. The nickname stuck for the rest of his life.

Though I had barely met Father's family, they proved to be particularly loving and kind to us after Father's death. Highlighting my childhood were the many packages that would come for us from the Goldsteins of New York, and what wonders they contained: sports equipment, new clothes, food and candy of all kinds—gifts that told us time and again that Father's family was thinking of us, that they would never abandon Murph's boys.

So much time had passed since I had last seen them. In the interim, my grandparents had died, but I was anxious to reunite with the rest of this big, boisterous, welcoming family once again. I decided to surprise them. Finding my way to New York City, I took the Brighton Beach Express subway from Times Square to Brooklyn and found my grandparents' house on East Seventeenth Street. Now living in my grandparents' home were my father's married sister Dora, her husband Al, and their two children, along with unmarried Uncle Phil and unmarried Aunt Libby.

Surrounded by loving uncles, aunts, and cousins (I am at the center, in uniform), it was hard to believe that I would soon be fighting for my life on a battlefield somewhere in Europe.

I rang the bell and waited. When Uncle Phil answered the door, there was a second or two of shocked silence as he took in the uniformed lad grinning down at him. Then came the joyful shout, "Ivan's here!" Everyone came running, crowding around me in a huge, tearful embrace.

Ivan's here! Word went out, and within a half hour, the whole family had bustled into the house. It was a wonderful and nostalgic reunion that lasted late into the night and continued the next day. That day was to be the last carefree day in my life for quite awhile.

Yom Kippur, September 27, 1944: Jews everywhere in the world are pouring out their hearts to the Almighty

Judge, the only power great enough to stop the merciless Nazi butchers. Men and women in concentration camps, broken by labor and starvation, pray silently, straining to remember the holy words, even as their tormentors force them to work yet harder on that day. Soldiers on the front, mothers and fathers back home, religious and nonreligious, rabbis and renegades, all weep and try to muster strength. And yes, Ivan Goldstein is praying.

Just before Yom Kippur eve, we were told that our division could ship out at a moment's notice. We were therefore confined to barracks, so that the entire division could be mobilized quickly. The only exception was permission for us to go to the mess hall at mealtimes. I realized that the mess hall was next to the chapel and that the Kol Nidrei service would be starting there soon, marking the beginning of the twenty-four-hour fast. I reasoned that since I wouldn't be going to eat in the mess hall, I should be able to attend the Yom Kippur services instead. My buddy, Jules Levine, didn't see it that way. "We're confined to barracks, Ivan," he countered. "If they give the order to move out and you're anywhere but in the barracks or mess hall, you could probably be court-martialed!" But going to the chapel on Yom Kippur was really important to me: so important that I cajoled Jules into cooperating. "If the order is given, you just run over and tell me. I'll be back before anyone misses me." He reluctantly agreed, and I went to services that night, and again the next day, poised to bolt to the barracks if I so much as saw Jules enter the chapel.

It was worth the risk, for I knew that my time of trial had come, that I was to face an enemy that was daring, desperate and hated me as both an American soldier and as a Jew. They would do all they could to vanquish this Jew along with the rest. Keenly aware of the danger before me, I was moved by the mournful, sobering liturgy, "On this day it is decreed, who shall live, and who shall die. . . ." But with the optimism of youth, I didn't allow myself to contemplate the horrors of war. I would go over there and do my best. The rest was up to God.

Right after Yom Kippur was over, the chaplain handed out boxed meals. Jewish women in the area, filled with compassion for the Jewish soldiers, had sent meals on which we could break our fast. The chicken dinner I received was fabulous, and I wrote to the woman who had prepared it to tell her how much it meant to me.

No sooner had I eaten than the order came for us to ship out. I was ready. We were rushed off the base and taken to New York. I stood on the deck of the ship, watching the harbor slip away. Our division was on two ships, the British HMS *Samaria* and the American USS *Hermitage,* each holding approximately five thousand men. When we left during the night, we had no idea that we were part of a massive military convoy. When dawn broke and we looked out over the sea, we realized that our ship was just one of a huge convoy of forty-eight American and British ships.

Ever since the successful invasion of Normandy on D-Day, June 6, 1944, Allied troops had been pushing the German occupation of Western Europe farther and farther back. But reinforcements were needed, and fresh artillery and airborne divisions had to be moved into place to finish off the stubborn enemy. The massive armada pulling out of New York was bound for Normandy, a trip that should have been a three- to four-day Atlantic crossing. But the Germans were well aware of us, and their U-boats dogged our ships, persistently trying to delay the inevitable landing. It took fourteen days to reach the European shore.

Six days out, however, the ship's captain informed us that because of heavy damage, the port at Normandy could not be used to unload the massive tanks of our division. My ship, the HMS *Samaria,* was diverted to Liverpool, and the *Hermitage* landed in Southampton. All the other ships of the convoy carried on to Normandy.

We stayed in England from mid-October until December 20, building up our physiques through hours of training, long hikes, and endless exercise. The sweat was worth it, though, for I left England stronger than I had ever been. I have no doubt that the strength and stamina I developed helped preserve my life during the trials that were to come.

A small incident comes to mind, insignificant maybe, but one that I enjoy remembering. As I had become known to my buddies as an artist, they often asked me to draw cartoons on their letters to give the folks back home a little laugh. In the military, all mail was censored before it went back to the States, and since my captain was our censor, he couldn't help noticing the cartoons.

One day, he called me into his office and remarked affably, "I had no idea you had such talent! I'd like you to draw a cartoon on my letter home." "I only do that for my friends," I answered.

Then I turned and left him with his letter dangling from his hand. Revenge? Maybe, but it sure felt good. I never claimed to be a *tzaddik* (a righteous person).

During occasional light moments like that, it was easy to forget that there was a war going on. But the war was real, very real to the citizens of Great Britain. Until I visited London, I had no idea how great the toll of war could be on a civilian population. When we had time off, my friends and I would go to see shows in this grand metropolis. London seemed to be the height of civilization; propriety ruled, and the orderliness of British society was grounded with a sense of security—until the Germans attacked.

Despite the mandatory blackouts, when the entire city went almost miraculously dark, the German V2 rockets found their targets. The V2 was the newest long-range German rocket. It carried two thousand pounds of explosives and took only minutes to reach its target from mobile launchers in Holland. The V2 was especially feared because it could not be shot down once it was in flight. No matter where you were, when the air raid sirens wailed, you ran for the bomb shelter as fast as you could, because the rocket could be over your head any second. Crowded into the shelters, we could hear the rockets come shrieking through the night, followed by loud explosions, and we could only imagine what devastation we would find when we emerged. It was too much for a Denver boy, but I was emboldened by the palpable determination of the Brits.

Ironically, one of my most frightening experiences of the war happened on the friendly British mainland, far from the battlefield. We were stationed in Warminster, where the rolling hills were perfect for practice driving the tanks. As night fell, a total blackout was observed, and in this blackness we were charged with guarding the hundreds of tanks parked on the hills, roughly two hundred yards from the barracks. Guard duty was no laughing matter. The task rotated from one soldier to the next, each shift lasting for three to four hours—walking around the tanks, watching for saboteurs. Alertness was critical, no matter what the hour. If a guard fell asleep, it was punishable by death, for the safety of all was at stake. You could not leave your post until another guard came to start his shift.

One night, it was my turn to go on guard duty, relieving the previous guard until my replacement would come at dawn. As soon as the door of the barracks shut behind me, I was in total darkness. It was raining hard, and there was no moon, no stars. I strained my eyes to see, but all was black. Trudging through the mud in the downpour, not seeing or hearing anything but the rain, I never felt so alone. No matter where I looked, there were no tanks. I became disoriented and looked again and again, but I couldn't find the tanks. I yelled to find the guard who was supposed to go off duty. No answer. The rain came down harder.

Screaming into the darkness, in mud up to my ankles, I wondered if falling asleep was punishable by death: what is the penalty for not relieving a guard? I wandered round and round, frantically trying to find the guard, the tanks, anything. Images of a court-martial and, oh God, firing squads hammered my brain. After what must have been an hour or two, I was exhausted. I sank into the mud and just cried. I stayed there, miserable and trembling, until the sun came up, until I was sure that, by now, someone else would be on his way to relieve the poor soul who had to stay on duty through two shifts. As the first shafts of light pierced the fog, I went back to the barracks, changed clothes, and went to sleep.

Remarkably, no one ever said anything to me about it. No one asked, no one told. There was no court-martial and no firing squad. But the incident unnerved me, and for the first time I wondered how I'd hold up in combat. Would I be immobilized by fear? I was soon to find out.

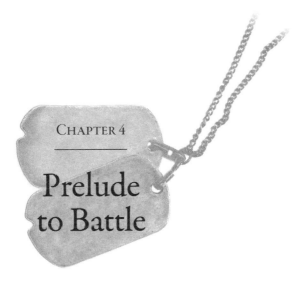

CHAPTER 4

Prelude to Battle

THE ALLIES HAD WRESTED CHERBOURG, a key port in France, from German control on June 25, almost six months to the day before we landed there in December. It had been hailed as the "gateway to victory" by triumphant Yanks, and it stood ready to receive us. We crossed the English Channel in LSTs, the enormous craft designed to hold tanks and men and land them safely on undeveloped shores. Although their crews called them "large, slow targets", the initials actually stood for "landing ship, tank." It was truly a marvel, invented specifically to transport tanks and equipment for this war. It was remarkably strong and buoyant, and few losses of LSTs are on record.

Cherbourg, where we landed in France, had been taken back by
the Allies after heavy fighting. *Official U.S. Army Photo*

From Cherbourg, we drove our tanks about 450 miles
eastward over the Seine River, through the outskirts of
Paris, bound for the town of Soissons. It was there that we
had our first taste of enemy fire. A German plane fired at us
and dropped a single bomb. This first encounter with the
enemy left some of us pretty unnerved. But we were told to
hide under the tanks and save our energy for the real fight
that was to come.

We were to take part in the now-famous Battle of
the Bulge. At this point in the war, Hitler had tasted
defeat repeatedly and had been backed into a corner.
The Allied armies were on his border, and he knew that
it was a matter of time—little time—before there would

be an all-out offensive to take Germany itself. His only hope was to push for a final attack against the Western Front. If he could cut through the Allied lines and reach Antwerp, he could effectively cut the Allied flank in two. For this critical von Rundstedt Offensive, Hitler personally planned every move and mustered a quarter of a million troops to take up positions on an eighty-five-mile line from southern Belgium to Luxembourg. His men advanced fifty miles into Allied territory, creating a fearsome "bulge" that cut deep into Allied defenses in the Ardennes region.

Unprepared for this aggressive onslaught, American commanders initially ignored the German troop movements reported to them. But after heavy initial losses, the Allied supreme commander, Gen. Dwight D. Eisenhower, called upon Gens. George Patton, Anthony McAullife, Omar Bradley, and other top military leaders to meet the brazen enemy with enormous numbers of men and arms—a half-million determined infantry, airmen, and artillerymen to effectively push back the bulge to the German border. Committing this many troops to what promised to be the biggest battle in U.S. history, Eisenhower felt confident that the massive thrust would help end the war soon.

British Field Marshal Bernard Montgomery wrangled with Eisenhower over command of the ground troops, and this dissension in the top circles of military leadership delighted the enemy. However, it was of little consequence to us, the rank-and-file recruits whose mission was to follow orders and plunge into battle. Our 11th Armored Division, nicknamed "Thunderbolts," was to play an important role in a battle that was to live on in Belgian memory for decades.

In the little town of Bastogne, a tense drama was unfolding, one that riveted the attention of the entire world. The German Wehrmacht had swept through the entire area, retaking Belgian lands that American forces had liberated in September. They conquered it all, except for centrally located Bastogne, where Gen. Anthony McAuliffe and his 101st Airborne Division were valiantly holding them off. With three German infantry divisions and a panzer (tank) division deployed around the town, the 101st was trapped. General Gerd von Runstedt sent an emissary to McAuliffe with a demand for surrender. At first, General McAullife wasn't sure whether the Germans were surrendering or whether he was being told to surrender. When it was clarified that it was the Americans who were to surrender, he replied, "Nuts!" and shooed the emissaries back to their commander. His reply was translated into German as "Go to Hell!"

McAuliffe's response made headlines around the world. With little left but the pluck of a besieged American officer, he had delivered a retort that carved his place in history. The impact was electrifying. It boosted morale for Allied troops on every front. War-weary civilians took heart that the triumph of good over evil was at hand. "Nuts!" became

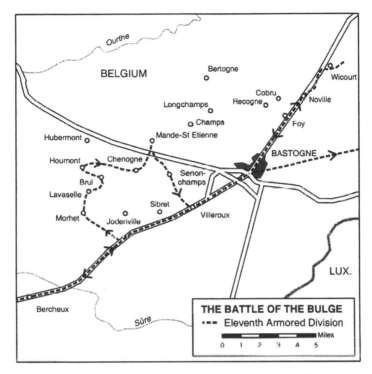

The arrows show the movements of the 11th Armored Division from our entrance into battle until after the Battle of the Bulge.

a rallying cry, and Bastogne became a symbol of resistance that captured the hearts of all.

Hitler vowed to take Bastogne, no matter what the cost. Determined to defend Bastogne and liberate the entire region, the Allies decided to push from the north and south, attempting to squeeze the Germans out of the area and push them back. Frigid December temperatures, the coldest in Western European memory, played a deadly role in the battles as well. Poorly dressed for constant below-zero temperatures, American troops were literally freezing to death as they spent night after night in icy foxholes and day after day advancing through whirling snow into heavy artillery fire. Even General Patton, known for his speed, was pushing his way toward Bastogne with maddening slowness.

Yet Patton managed to reach Bastogne just one day after his confident prediction. By December 27, the German encirclement of the town was broken, and the bulge had been contained. But now the grim assignment to push the Germans back was just beginning. There were many miles to cover, and even though the American tanks outnumbered the German tanks by ten to one, the Germans had superior guns and had hunkered down in towns and villages to withstand the bitter cold. Moreover, Hitler had refused his own generals' desperate pleas to allow their retreat. Attempts to retreat would be punished by firing squad. They were there to fight to the death.

We had driven our tanks through France and crossed over into Belgium. The extreme cold covered the fields with ice and snow, causing hazardous driving for a vehicle with metal tracks such as ours. You might say we slid into Belgium. And temperatures were dropping again.

On the night of December 29, 1944, our Company B, 41st Tank Battalion of the 11th Armored Division, moved up to a bivouac area in Longlier, Belgium. The company was assembled that night after dinner, and we

Snow covered the ground as we prepared to rumble toward battle in our Shermans. *Official U.S. Army Photo*

were informed that we were going into battle the next day. We were briefed that the plan was to attack north of Morhet with the object of destroying the enemy positions at Lavaselle (approximately eight miles west of Bastogne). We were told how the 101st Airborne Division was occupying Bastogne, still locked in a fierce battle with the encircling Germans. The Battle of the Bulge had been raging for two weeks, and the German resistance was fierce. The shivers going through our bones on this sub-zero night reminded us that freezing to death was a very real and gruesome possibility.

We also knew that the outcome of the war could depend on defeating the Germans' last massive effort, planned by der Führer himself. "German morale and supplies are running low," we were told. "Their men are shot as deserters if they try to retreat. They must continue fighting, even when all is lost, so they are desperate men. Moreover, some of them are wearing American uniforms, so pay attention to passwords. It could save your life."

Our captain explained the battle plan to us in crisp, businesslike tones, as if he were sending his men into war games instead of a battlefield from which some would never return. Then he warmed to the subject, telling us that this would be our "baptism of fire," that we must fight hard to defend the world from evil, and that America and the world were watching. We were all inspired by McAuliffe's stand against the Germans.

That night, I cleared the snow from a small patch on the ground and unrolled my sleeping bag. But sleep was impossible. My thoughts were totally absorbed with the coming battle. Questions I had been afraid to ask myself now flooded my mind in wave after terrible wave: How would I react to combat? Would I remember my training? Was my training good enough? Could I really kill another human being? Would I be killed? What if I'm wounded or captured? Would I be brave?

I must have fallen asleep, because I felt myself wake much before dawn. I rolled up my sleeping bag and tried to prepare myself for the challenge of the coming day. Suddenly, I recalled a brief conversation when I left home for induction. My mother had said, "Be sure to take your tefillin." These are small leather boxes holding scrolls of Bible verses worn during morning prayers.

"Mom, they get us up early in the morning; I certainly won't have time to put on tefillin and say morning prayers!"

"Ivan," she replied archly, "there will come a special time, or maybe times when it will be possible." Her voice softened. "Just take them," she pleaded.

Thinking back to that conversation, I decided that now was the special time she envisioned. I returned my sleeping bag to the tank, took my tefillin from my duffel bag, and discreetly went into a forested area about fifty yards away. It was freezing cold, snowing, and black. I removed my jacket and placed the tefillin on my left arm and on my head. They were like old friends, comforting to the touch and subtly uplifting. I began my morning prayers, first reciting the standard prayers that I knew by heart. But I soon found myself in a very intent dialogue with God. "Please save me, protect me, give me the strength I'll need. . . ."

The fast-approaching events again filled my mind. I knew that all the training in the world would be of no use if God were not watching over me. In my mind, it was a true dialogue, for it seemed to me that God was listening

59

and indeed would not let down Ida's son. After all, He had been her "Partner" throughout my childhood; would He abandon us now?

Light of day was breaking, and the members of the company were waking. I gave my tefillin one last kiss, stuffed them back in their little velvet bag, and rushed back to my tank. After we ate our K-rations for breakfast, there were brief instructions, and soon the air was filled with the heavy roar of tank after tank rolling across the snowy fields. We were on the move toward Lavaselle.

CHAPTER 5

Baptism of Fire

T HERE WAS NO TIME FOR FEAR. We were headed for combat, and a healthy tension was palpable inside our M4 Sherman tank. There were five of us. In the lower section sat the driver, Andrew Urda from Michigan, an amiable, jovial person, and the assistant driver/bow gunner (me), operating a .30-caliber machine gun. In the turret was the gunner, Cpl. Cecil Peterman from Oklahoma, with a 75mm canon. A quiet and withdrawn person, Peterman was always neat and spotless. His hobby was making state-of-the-art, original hunting knives, and he carried one of his creations on him at all times. The loader, Pvt. Dage Hebert, had worked on a farm in Montana, and by nature he was a helpful and friendly person. Staff

Sergeant Wallace Alexander was our able tank commander. Young and striking in appearance, he was an aspiring actor from New York. Before the war, he attended Columbia University's Drama School and had acted in a number of plays. My impression of Wally was that he was the best tank commander in the company, including the officers, and that I

Staff Sergeant Wallace Alexander, commander.

was fortunate to be part of his crew. And I was particularly glad not to be in the companion tank commanded by my captain.

So there we were, as diverse a group as you could imagine, from all parts of the country, bound together in a single objective: to join the battle as courageous American soldiers, and, hopefully, to come out of it alive.

We had named our tank *Barracuda,* and as resident artist, I painted the name on it. We were attached to General Patton's Third Army. The operation was code-named Poker because the battalion commander, Lt. Col. Wray F. Sagaser, was renowned as a poker player. Though I never saw Patton, I was well aware of his reputation. A daring general and a hard fighter, his theory was to take the enemy as fast as you can, no matter what the losses. The main thing was to win.

I learned later that other military leaders had objected to his putting the 11th Armored Division into action on that day, December 30, because many of us were exhausted from the long, freezing, overland trek of the days before, and because the artillery and infantry support deemed necessary for a successful attack had not yet arrived. Patton didn't care. He sent us in anyway, despite his peers' dismal predictions of heavy losses. In fact, the condition of 11th Armored aside, there were more casualties at the Bulge than in any other battle in American history.

At the time, we were unaware of our slim chances. Following orders, glad to be headed for action at last, we turned north on the road toward Morhet. We had two platoons in line and one in reserve. We moved easily through the northern edge of the village. When we left the road, heading into the fields, we heard the first sounds of German gunfire. This was it! The curtain was rising on the "big show."

Our radio crackled: "Engaged in battle, 7:30 a.m., the Krauts are on the run!" As we came to the crest of the hill, I spotted a lone German soldier riding a bicycle as fast as he could in the valley below. I watched through my periscope as machine-gun fire from the tanks to my left ripped through the terrain, finally reaching the soldier on the bike—the first enemy casualty. Just like that. Alive one second; dead the next.

A wave of nausea welled up inside me. This was the enemy, I told myself earnestly. A German, a Nazi, a barbarian. We had been told awful things about the way the Krauts treated American prisoners, so we would be better fighters and be jubilant when we killed them. I just felt sick.

I had been too young at my father's death to grasp its dread finality. In fact, my first meaningful brush with death had been when I was about twelve years old. A childhood friend, Louis Weicker, shared my love of drawing, and we used to spend hours together, sketching and creating what we deemed great art. Even as a child, he had inspired me, subtly pushing me to compete with his outstanding talent. We vowed to be fellow artists and lifelong friends. But right after we graduated together from elementary school, Lou became ill, deathly ill. It didn't seem possible; it didn't seem right. We were going to be buddies forever. When he passed away, I felt like a part of me—a joyous, creative part of me—had died with him.

But now, here on this barren battlefield, it was different. I was facing vicious, desperate soldiers, I thought resolutely. They were expertly trained to kill me, unless I could get them first. I should be glad to see their blood staining the frozen ground; I should be glad.

We rolled down into the valley. The barn in front of us was the next objective, and I pictured it full of enemy fighters. Our tanks hit the barn with an avalanche of firepower. The barn doors flew open, but instead of German soldiers, horses and cows came stampeding from the barn with blood spurting from their sides like fountains—whinnying, bellowing, writhing in the snow. Somehow, I hadn't expected this, and I was shocked by it. More nausea.

The battle plan required moving across open fields to our targets. *Official U.S. Army Photo*

But a growing sense of victory kept me going. For the next two or three hours, Company B's offensive was going forward at full speed. We must have surprised the enemy by the first stages of our attack, for we met with little resistance. We swept through a number of villages, taking prisoners, demolishing buildings, and destroying houses that shielded enemy fire. Later in the morning, we were supported by a squadron of our air force P-47s, which strafed enemy vehicles and troops in front of us. By early afternoon, we had liberated a number of villages and farm communities.

We left a village, heading for the open road toward Lavaselle, following the company commander's tank. We then realized that our two tanks had become separated

from the rest of the company.
It was around 3:00 p.m. when
a voice shouted over the radio,
"We've been hit!"

Urda yelled, "They got the
captain's tank!"

Alone behind a barn, we
suddenly felt a jolt at the
back of our tank and heard a
loud explosion. We had been

Sergeant Andrew Urda,
driver.

hit too, but we could still move, and Urda drove around
the barn, headed toward the snow-covered valley below.
We were surrounded. Shells exploded all around us. Urda
headed for what he thought was a patch of open ground,
but it turned out to be a snow-covered lake, and the
Barracuda quickly came to a stop. The harder he tried to
maneuver and free the vehicle, the deeper it became mired
in the mud and water.

We were sitting ducks. Almost immediately, the
Barracuda's left side was struck with a powerful German
88mm shell. The tank was on fire. Behind my seat, there
was an escape hatch leading out through the bottom of the
tank. A square wooden ammunition box filled with candy
bars and chewing gum was on top of the hatch. These were
rations that I had saved up after hearing that there would
be no candy rations in battle. My sweet-tooth stash would
soon go up in flames, and the ammunition in the tank
would soon catch fire as well. In a flash, I decided it was

We rolled through some small towns, defeating any resistance we met and liberating the citizens. *Official U.S. Army photo*

better to take my chances getting out of the tank than to be inside when the ammo exploded.

But the candy box blocked my reach to the release lever. Water was coming in through the bottom of the tank anyway, so escape below the tank was impossible. I did the only thing I could: I raised the hatch above my head and jumped out through the top. Running across the top of the tank toward the rear, I could hear a nonstop stream of machine-gun fire striking the metal below me.

I leaped off the tank into the icy water and tried to tread as far way from the tank as possible. Under the water, I held out for as long as I could, hoping the Germans would be satisfied with the burning tank and leave. After what seemed like a long time—but actually could only have been only a few minutes—I raised my head for air. My heart sank as I saw that half a dozen smirking German soldiers were right there, their weapons pointed at me. I climbed out of the pond with my hands raised. A gun was rammed into my back, guiding me away from the *Barracuda,* which was now a raging pyre.

Corporal Cecil Peterman, gunner.

A few yards away, I spotted one of our crew face-down in the snow, with blood oozing from a large, open wound in his back. I knew immediately it was Peterman. Seeing the hunting knife attached to his belt, a German soldier turned him over to open his belt and remove the knife, and then I could see poor Peterman's grotesque facial wound. Blood was pouring out of his cheek, and I figured he must be dead. About fifteen yards in front of the tank, Andy Urda was standing with his hands raised, and near him, Wally Alexander was lying in the snow, writhing in pain from massive leg wounds. Hebert was nowhere to be seen.

A German brought a large blanket and ordered Andy and me to lift Alexander on it and carry him up the hill to a large farmhouse on the other side of the valley. About twenty-five yards from the farmhouse, we were told to put him down and wait. Wally was in great pain and crying that his legs were freezing and that he was losing the feeling in them. The water on my clothes had frozen, and I was chilled to the bone. I felt pain in my leg too: pain I hadn't noticed before. Looking down at my thigh, I saw a rip in my pants with blood around it. Apparently,

Private Ivan Goldstein, assistant driver and bow gunner.

the Germans were not the poor marksmen I thought they were. While I was running along the tank, a bullet must have ripped my pant leg, causing a flesh wound in my thigh. I immediately applied a field pack bandage to my wound. (Every soldier is equipped with basic bandaging supplies before battle. We carried these on us but optimistically thought that we'd never need them.)

Wally was in bad shape and screaming for help. Andy and I applied field-pack bandages to his wounds, and we took turns massaging his legs to bring back the circulation. But his pathetic cries and pleas continued. In my earlier army life, I had been confidently forward with people, never fearing rank or authority. Now was no different. I went to the guard standing a short distance from us, and asked for medical aid for Wally.

Annoyed at my boldness, he merely pointed to the ground and told me to sit back down. They must have

left the three of us sitting in
the frozen snow for almost
two hours; it was getting
dark. We did our best to
encourage each other and
comfort Wally, but deep
down we seriously ques-
tioned whether any of us
would live to tell about
this. Finally, some soldiers
came and carried Wally Alexander away. We wondered if
Peterman was just badly wounded or actually dead, and
where on this miserable planet was Hebert?

Private Dage Hebert,
loader.

In any case, it was just Andy and me now. A
guard led us to a small shed and put us inside. To our
surprise, there were three American soldiers sitting
on the ground in there. One was from our company:
Technician 4th Class Ed Mattson, the driver of the
captain's tank. He told us that when their tank was hit,
the other four in his crew were killed immediately and
never got out of the tank. He was the lone survivor. His
hand was covered with a blood-soaked rag, and he was
in agonizing pain.

It was strange to think that my captain—the man who
had despised me throughout training—had died that
day. I don't recall feeling any kind of elation at the news.
My mind was preoccupied with my own problem. But
awareness that someone I had known so well had been

70

killed made death seem that much closer. It could happen to anyone of any rank, any disposition, any background. Death doesn't care who you are.

The other two Americans in the shed were paratroopers from the 101st Airborne Division. They had been in a foxhole on the outskirts of Bastogne, posted to keep watch for German infiltrators, when Germans sneaked up from behind and captured them. They introduced themselves as Ed Lozano and Ed Kessler. None of us had eaten all day. In the thick of battle, you don't notice hunger, but now that we were sitting around, waiting for something to happen, we began to count the hours since we had last eaten.

The outfits we wore were a flimsy match for the frigid weather. I was particularly chilled because of my dip in the lake. We noticed that the Germans were wearing fleece-lined jackets. Hitler had learned his lesson in the battle for Moscow in 1941. His victorious advance in Russia had brought him within nineteen miles of Moscow when the arctic Russian winter stopped his elite troops in their tracks. The embattled Soviet forces were saved by fresh Siberian troops, well outfitted for winter warfare. Hitler now knew only too well that to win this war, his army must be able to withstand extreme weather conditions. Knowing that the Americans were badly equipped to handle frigid weather, he had waited for brutal December conditions to launch his offensive in the Ardennes region. We were now victims of his strategy: it would only be a matter of time before the sub-zero winds would take our lives, if a bullet didn't do the job first.

A guard opened the door of the shed, ordered Urda and Lozano to follow him, and relocked the door as they left. About forty minutes later, they returned, and the guard took Kessler and me. The farmhouse had been turned into the German headquarters. We entered through the front door, went up a few steps to the left, and then I was ordered to sit at the desk of the German major. Kessler sat in a chair against the wall, waiting next in line. The officer ordered me to stand and had his assistant remove the contents of my pockets. Speaking in a chummy manner in perfect English, with hardly an accent, he said that he had been living in Forest Hills, New York, before the war. "I hear that Al Smith died," he began jovially, referring to the one-time presidential candidate. I stood stiffly at attention and answered that I hadn't read a newspaper lately. From the contents of my pockets that were sitting on his desk, he picked up a letter from my mother that I had received some days before.

Like a flashing red light, I suddenly recalled a deadly sentence in that letter. It was "Ivan, I hope that you received the package I sent you for Chanukah." Moreover, my dog tags had the letter H on them, for "Hebrew." The stories that I had heard about the German concentration camps and what Hitler was doing to the Jews of Europe raced through my mind, and a quiet panic gripped me. The major looked at me, and his countenance turned somber as he clenched his jaw. He spoke.

"Private Goldstein, I see that you are Jewish." I didn't answer.

"Your tank partner, Urda, is also Jewish," he added menacingly.

"No, sir, Sergeant Urda is Catholic!"

"He looks Jewish!"

"OK, I'm Jewish," I said earnestly, "but Andy's not! He's really not."

In truth, Andy appeared more Jewish than I did. His parents were Slovaks, and he was devoutly Catholic, yet somehow he had a Jewish look. The major assumed he had switched dog tags with someone else.

I don't know if my assertion changed the major's mind about Andy, but at least it introduced enough of a doubt for him to let it go. He turned to his assistant and spoke in German, not realizing that the paratrooper Ed Kessler came from a German family background and understood his instructions: "In the morning, take the Jew out and shoot him."

To the major's surprise, Kessler spoke up: "You can't do that! You can't shoot an American prisoner! It's against the Geneva Conventions." The treaties signed in Geneva formulated rules of international war, particularly regarding the treatment of prisoners of war and captured noncombatants.

Unimpressed with Kessler's truly brave outburst, the major's icy reply was, "Be quiet, or I'll add you to the list."

After Kessler's interrogation, we were taken back to the shed and locked in. Mattson was no longer there. I feared for his life, but Andy said he was taken away for treatment of his hand wound. We had no way of knowing the truth.

My fate, however, was clear. I was to be executed in the morning, despite the official "rules" of war. There seemed to be no escape from our tiny jail, but everyone urged me to try to get out. My head ached. I looked at the walls, studied the ground, and considered breaking down the door. But nothing even remotely possible came to mind. Finally, we decided that if the door opened again, I should make a break for it and run toward the nearest forest. I had always been a pretty fast runner, and though I was starved and cold, I figured that if they were caught off guard for a few seconds, I might be able to outrun them. It wasn't much of a plan, but at least it was better than the certain death awaiting me.

I didn't think about hunger and cold the rest of the night; I was waiting—poised to run if that door would open. But in the middle of the night, the sound of exploding artillery shells, distant at first, became louder and louder. What was happening?

Just outside our shed, we could hear the sputter of motors starting up and then the sounds of vehicles moving in every direction, German commands, shouts, and running feet. The commotion lasted for the next hour; then, suddenly the noise, motors, and voices stopped. The artillery barrage continued, ever nearer, in salvos. Another fifteen minutes passed and our door was opened.

Two guards hurried in. "Get up! Get up! We must leave!" they commanded. We figured it out in an instant. The Americans, our good ol' Yanks, had started an offensive during the night, God bless them. They were advancing rapidly toward our position, Hubermont and the Rechrival Valley. The German command had evacuated earlier, anticipating the American attack.

The guard brought out a large, heavy backpack of supplies. "This is for the Jew to carry," he announced. "He must carry it himself. Do not try to help him!" He strapped it to my back and marched us out. My execution had been cancelled, or at least postponed. I trudged along carrying the backpack, but in my heart, I was giving thanks for the miracle that had saved me.

The end of my first and only day in battle had come and gone.

CHAPTER 6

Captivity

W E WERE WALKING EASTWARD, toward Germany, marching continuously till daybreak. I wondered if I would ever see my family again. What would happen if I collapsed in the snow, unable to go on? What if that guard decided to pull the trigger? Would my mother ever find out what happened to me? Poor Mom! She's such a worrier. How will she react when she doesn't hear from me?

I had no way of knowing that, in fact, my mother was somewhat aware of my situation. Her deep empathy with people she loved gave her sort of a psychic hotline of information—dreams that were uncannily true. Throughout my life, I would be skeptical of some awful dream she had, only to find out that it had been eerily prophetic. There was the time she dreamt about Mrs. Finley, an Irish lady who worked near the store. Long conversations and shared confidences had bound them as friends. One night, Mother dreamt that she was visiting Mrs. Finley in the hospital and that her friend's leg was black and swollen. In the morning, we told her not to trouble herself about it; after all, everyone has bad dreams once in a while. But Mother was deeply concerned. The next day, the phone call came. It was from Mrs. Finley, calling from the hospital. She had fallen off a ladder and badly injured her leg.

At just about the time that I was captured, Mother had another one of her dreams, the kind that seemed so real that she would awake with her heart pounding. She confided the dream to my brothers.

"I saw Ivan," she told them tearfully. "I saw Ivan jumping through flames!"

"Mom, it was only a dream. Don't worry about it," they told her.

"But I saw it—he was leaping through a fire. I couldn't tell if it was from a burning building, but it was some kind of structure. He was trying to escape. He was jumping, running through flames. . . ."

They could say nothing to console her. Mother had last heard from me when I wrote her a letter from France, around December 26. On January 18, at about 8:00 p.m., Max had just begun a session with Mr. Herzel, a tutor Mother had hired to supplement his Jewish studies. Mother was cooking in the kitchen when the doorbell rang. She opened the front door and was handed a Western Union telegram. She opened it with shaking hands.

A horrible shriek coming from the living room brought Max and Mr. Herzel rushing in. Mother had collapsed into her rocking chair, crying and screaming, with the telegram clutched in her hand. It was from the adjutant general in Washington, D.C., notifying her that Pfc. Ivan Goldstein was listed as missing in action as of December 30.

Mr. Herzel tried to console her, reassuring her over and over that I was probably alive. Jerry (who was married by now) was called, and he hurried to our house to calm his hysterical mother.

After I shipped out, I had made it a point to send my letters to the store, for I knew Mother would see them earlier in the day than if I sent them home. Jerry was at Murph's before her every morning, and he would sift through the day's mail.

As weeks dragged into months, the first question she always asked as she walked through the door was, "Any news about Ivan? Any letters?"

"No."

"No telegrams?"

"No. Nothing at all."

"I guess only God knows where he is. We'll just have to wait a little longer."

She never gave up hope, even when the war seemed practically over and there was still no word, even when everyone

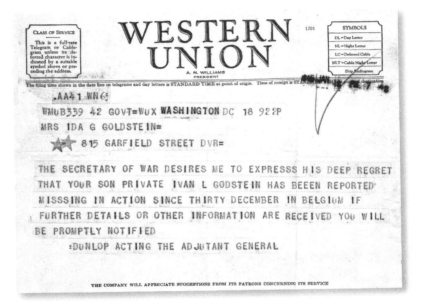

On January 18, 1945, more than two weeks after I was captured, Mother received this telegram.

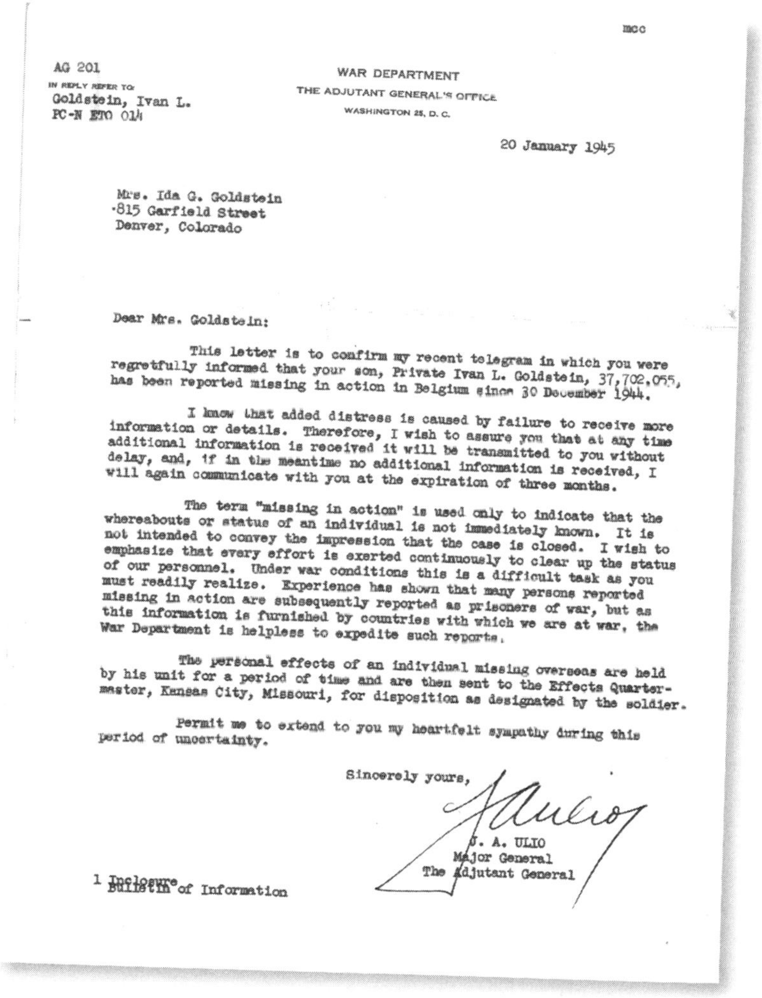

mcc

AG 201
IN REPLY REFER TO:
Goldstein, Ivan L.
PC-N ETO 014

WAR DEPARTMENT
THE ADJUTANT GENERAL'S OFFICE
WASHINGTON 25, D. C.

20 January 1945

Mrs. Ida G. Goldstein
815 Garfield Street
Denver, Colorado

Dear Mrs. Goldstein:

This letter is to confirm my recent telegram in which you were regretfully informed that your son, Private Ivan L. Goldstein, 37,702,055, has been reported missing in action in Belgium since 30 December 1944.

I know that added distress is caused by failure to receive more information or details. Therefore, I wish to assure you that at any time additional information is received it will be transmitted to you without delay, and, if in the meantime no additional information is received, I will again communicate with you at the expiration of three months.

The term "missing in action" is used only to indicate that the whereabouts or status of an individual is not immediately known. It is not intended to convey the impression that the case is closed. I wish to emphasize that every effort is exerted continuously to clear up the status of our personnel. Under war conditions this is a difficult task as you must readily realize. Experience has shown that many persons reported missing in action are subsequently reported as prisoners of war, but as this information is furnished by countries with which we are at war, the War Department is helpless to expedite such reports.

The personal effects of an individual missing overseas are held by his unit for a period of time and are then sent to the Effects Quartermaster, Kansas City, Missouri, for disposition as designated by the soldier.

Permit me to extend to you my heartfelt sympathy during this period of uncertainty.

Sincerely yours,

J. A. ULIO
Major General
The Adjutant General

1 Inclosure
Bulletin of Information

The telegram was soon followed by a more personal letter.

around her began to whisper that Ivan would probably never come home. Mother continued to pray, trusting that somehow she would hear good news someday.

She pinned her hopes on a thin strand of encouragement extended to her from an unexpected source. My ex-roommate from ASTP, Richard Grossman, wound up as a medic in the 11th Armored Division. While I was in Camp Cooke, he was training as a medic at Fitzsimons Army Hospital near Denver, and he enjoyed many a meal with my family.

By the time Richard heard that my tank crew was missing, the Americans had recaptured the area where the tank sat in that frozen bog. He made a special trip to the vicinity and found the *Barracuda*; it bore clear marks of the shells that had pierced it and the fire that had ravaged the interior. He examined the tank carefully, looking for bodies, searching for anything that would reveal my fate. He could picture my mother and knew what she must be going through. Richard's innate kindness and gratitude to our family made him determined to send her some optimistic news, something that might cheer her.

So Richard wrote to Mother from Belgium. "I found Ivan's tank," he told her, "and the good news is that there are no bodies. The crew was probably taken alive. I'm sure you'll hear from the Red Cross very soon." For that simple, caring act, Richard became a hero to Mother and my family forever. He had sent her a tiny glimmer of light, when all around her was dark and foreboding. She had "seen" me jumping from my burning tank, and bolstered by Richard's note, she persistently held onto the belief that she would see me again, alive and well.

Fortunately, she couldn't see her Ivan now, a prisoner of war—a Jewish prisoner of war—being led into the German version of Hell. The four of us—Kessler, Lozano, Urda, and me—and our German guard marched for hours through the blistering cold. The pack was very heavy, but my rigorous training and exercise in England had made me hardy enough to endure it. At least the physical activity helped reduce the pain from my leg wound and the freezing weather.

Finally, we stopped for a rest at a village farmhouse, where the guard was replaced and the backpack removed. Our new guards had an additional twelve American prisoners with them, and I searched their faces to see if any of them were from my division. No, it was nobody I knew. We continued our march, still with no food.

One of the new prisoners whispered to me, "Whatever you do, don't stop; don't say you can't go on." They had just experienced such an episode. One of the prisoners could not continue; he was summarily taken to the side of the road and shot on the spot. I passed this information on to our foursome.

I have no idea how many hours passed, but my next recollection is of reaching the city of Prüm, Germany. We stopped at a building occupied by German soldiers, and we literally collapsed when we got inside. We were brought food—a slice of dark bread and a bowl of hot soup consisting of water, flour, and potato peelings. This delicacy—"potato peel soup"—was to be the staple food of our captivity, served once a day.

The warmth of the room and the hot soup gave me a new feeling of life. While I was sitting on the floor, savoring my meal, a tall German soldier came and stood next to me. I stand six feet three inches, and he must have been about that height too. He placed his foot next to my tanker boot, and seeing that it was his size, he ordered me to remove my boots.

"Can't," I said nonchalantly, "I need them."

In a split second, his gun was at my forehead. I set down my soup quickly and removed my beautiful boots as fast as I could. After he took the boots, he spotted my watch and pulled it off my wrist. I was left with only a double pair of socks covering my feet. I realized that I needed to put something around my feet or they would freeze. No one seemed to notice as I got up and walked into the next room, which turned out to be the kitchen. A soldier was busy washing dishes. I opened a door and found a closet with mops, brooms, and a large barrel of cleaning rags. I grabbed two armfuls of rags, stuck them under my jacket, and returned to the other room.

Finding the rags almost immediately after losing my shoes seemed to me an incredible coincidence. Though not on the miraculous scale of the American offensive canceling my certain execution, it was still a bit of divine providence, I reassured myself. I pulled the blessed rags out of my jacket and layered my feet with them. I tied the extra rags together and wrapped them around my waist as my reserve supply of "shoes."

The POWs were taken outside to a barn where there were other American soldiers locked up for the night. The weather was still freezing, well below zero, and there was no heat in the barn. Many of the Americans were sick and suffering from exposure, and practically all of them had dysentery.

I sat with Andy and the paratroopers, Kessler and Lozano, hunched in a small circle. Grimly assessing our chances of survival at nearly zero, we were morose, to say the least. In a desperate situation like this, most people develop an attitude of "every man for himself." If I see a piece of bread, it's mine, even if I have to fight for it. But it seemed to me that a mindset like that would mean certain death for all of us, so I proposed the absurd idea of sharing. "Look," I said, "as individuals, we'll never make it. We have to become pairs—Andy and I can be one pair, and you guys are the other pair. Each person in the pair should be responsible for the other. Your other half has to be an extension of you." Then I waited.

They looked at each other, then at me. Their expressions were of mixed fear, desperation, and hope. I think, deep inside, they wondered whether they really would be capable of sharing their only crust of bread, of helping a partner, even if it meant defying our captors. "Guys, it's our only chance." I urged. "Let's make a pact."

I explained how the pairs would benefit each other: At night, we must hold each other close, using shared body heat to stay warm. For part of the night, one will hug the other person's back, and then we'll reverse, back and forth, during the night. Any food one of us gets, outside of given meals, must be shared with his partner. If one of the pair has trouble walking, the other will give his support. We need to think of ourselves as one person. If he's hurt, I'm hurt. If there's any chance for escape, we escape together.

They agreed to the pact, and we all made the solemn pledge.

The next morning was New Year's Day, 1945. The prisoners were divided into two work groups of approximately fourteen men each, with two guards assigned to a group. I noticed that all the guards were considerably older or younger than the combat soldiers: apparently the German army had a shortage of men. That was encouraging. Maybe the war would end soon.

We were given a series of jobs, helping on the nearby farms, repairing bombed railroad tracks, clearing debris from bombed-out buildings, and searching for victims of the air raids. Because of the unrelenting winter cold and sickness, prisoners died every night too, and burial detail was the grisliest job of all. We knew that using prisoners of war as slave laborers doing these kinds of tasks was against established international laws. But you don't speak up about your legal rights when guns are aimed straight at you.

One day, I was sent out with four other prisoners to work on a farm. There were no men there—all drafted into the German army, I suppose—and the person in charge was a woman between twenty and thirty years old. She was large in size, about two hundred pounds, and built like a football linebacker, with arms like a weight lifter. One of our jobs was filling sacks with potatoes and carrying and stacking the bags. It took two of us to lift and carry each sack, but our muscular fraülein would hoist a bag onto her shoulder and carry it by herself. It was clear she despised American weaklings.

I spotted a large tub of turnips nearby. Unnoticed, I managed to fill my pockets with them. I knew Andy and the paratroopers would be glad to receive this present. Anything edible was the greatest gift of all.

Working on labor details and tramping down the roads, we noticed that the supply trucks going toward the front revealed the great German war secret—that severe shortages were taking their toll on their war effort. The German military had cleverly circumvented their shortage of gasoline by developing an alternative-fuel engine. The first time we saw it, none of us could figure out what it was.

"Hey, look at that!" Urda said, pointing to a vehicle that had just passed us on the road.

"What?" I asked.

"That contraption strapped to the truck."

"I don't know. Smells like a fireplace."

"Will you look at that! They've got that truck running on a wood-burning engine!"

Though the invention was ingenious, we knew that it meant that the Germans were at the end of their supplies. That, and the obvious shortage of men, uplifted us—we dared to hope for liberation.

By this time, all the prisoners' bodies and clothes were infested with lice. Body, beard, hair, and clothes became breeding grounds for the biting lice and their eggs. At night, before falling into an exhausted sleep, we spent much of the time picking lice from ourselves. It was almost instinctive, like scratching a rash, and became a constant and unending part of life.

Like every other captive, I became an expert on lice, so here's some information that I hope will never be relevant to you: You can't kill lice by squeezing or crushing them with your fingers. You have to place them on your thumbnail and crush them with your other thumbnail. There are some things you never forget.

Our nightly conversations almost always revolved around food cravings, our favorite family meals, and the foods we missed most. Number one on my list was my mother's brisket, and I could picture it dripping with warm gravy. It's amazing how hunger changes even basic human nature, and I noticed it almost right away. In normal army life, sex was always a major topic. But as POWs, when survival was all we could think about, sex was never mentioned. Food—luscious, hot, American food—filled our dreams.

We held tenaciously to our plan of surviving in pairs. Nuzzled together at night, working side by side during the day, Andy and I shared our life stories. We talked incessantly about our families, about growing up, about our most personal memories, and above all, our plans for the future, "when this is over." Barely out of childhood, I confided how much my mother meant to me; how she had raised my brothers and me alone; how she had supported us and trained us to be upstanding citizens; how she imbued us with a love of reading and music, religion, and art. Andy would tell me, "The one person I must meet, more than anyone else after the war, is your mother!"

In normal times, I doubt if Andy and I ever would have become friends. But now—wrought by our common jeopardy and subhuman treatment—an unbreakable bond was forming. We were developing a rare closeness, and this relationship became one that I would never share with another human. Our survival depended upon each other, and our lives were united. We counted ourselves as fortunate as we managed to live out one more day. For Andy especially, it was important to put up a good front, not to let our German captors know how much we were suffering, not to let them think that the Yanks were cowards or weaklings. And somehow, trying to make the Germans think we were tough helped us believe it too.

One incident I will never forget. Our work group was marched out to railroad tracks near the edge of Prüm, to help repair a bombed-out section of track. This was not unusual, for one of General Eisenhower's main strategies was to keep supplies and munitions from reaching the Germans' western front. Our air force was blowing up every large German transport vehicle to keep it from getting to its destination, and this included blowing up trains and keeping the tracks unusable.

As POWs, we would come to know this fact in the worst way. We had just started our labor, when American planes dove down on the work crew, strafing and bombing the project. They made two passes. I jumped behind a large boulder near the tracks, but I was hit by some flying shrapnel in my left shin. I judged the wound to be minor. Quickly, I searched out my partner, Urda. He was OK. Two of the German workers and six of the Americans were dead, and we were all pretty shaken by the attack. We were to find out in the months to come that one of the great dangers to the POW labor gangs were our own Allied air forces.

For me, the Allied strafing was traumatic. At such a time, your powers of observation and your memory mechanisms are in high gear. The experience stays within you, even when your mind consciously snuffs it out. Even years later, the sound of planes would send me into a cold sweat. True fear—uncontrollable, irrational fear—would overtake me.

After the incident at the track, we were taken back to Prüm. The next day, new prisoners arrived, and we were on the march again, this time headed for the prison camp in Gerolstein. Our hope was that the next destination would be an improvement. Little did we know what was in store for us.

CHAPTER 7

The
Hellhole

WELCOME TO THE HELLHOLE" was the greeting we got from the inmates at Gerolstein. (Ironically, today the town is a health resort.) Few events stand out as vividly in my mind as our arrival there. There must have been five hundred to seven hundred prisoners of war in the huge, barn-like building, similar in structure to an airplane hangar. It was an enormous, drafty, open space with steel walls and cement floors. There was no heat, of course, and freezing from the severe cold was still a threat. Pneumonia was rampant, and there were no medicines.

Next to the hangar was another building; a single room with a large pit covered by wooden planks. Holes were cut in the planks for toilets. We were led there first, before joining the other inmates. The awful smell emanating from this outhouse sickened me instantly.

The entire area was enclosed with barbed wire. We were led into the hangar just before dark and served the usual potato peel soup and dark bread. At night the building was locked up and the outhouse wasn't available. Large forty- or fifty-gallon drums were spread out across the area's floor. These were the toilets for the night, with large stacks of coarse, newsprint-quality paper next to the drums. I don't know if the conscious objective was to dehumanize us, to make us feel that we were no more than animals penned up in this deplorable place, but these conditions quickly did the job.

All of the prisoners had dysentery. By morning, the many latrine barrels were filled to the rim, and the worst detail you could get was being assigned to move the barrels to the outhouse. It took three or four men to slide or lift the drums to their destination, and it was the filthiest task you could imagine. Andy and I were very fortunate in never having to work on this detail.

Other details were horrific in other ways. In the morning, we always found that eight or ten POWs had died during the night. The morning burial detail was also a terrible assignment, but it was a job that we could not avoid. We lifted each corpse onto a large wagon, and the wagon was pulled to a nearby field. There, we dumped them into a large common grave. At times, we felt sure that one day we would be the ones dumped into that hole. It was only a matter of time.

Somehow, the dead soldiers were always replaced by new POWs arriving in the camp. The new guys, though horrified and miserable in these dismal conditions, at least gave us hope. They brought news from the front, and the picture was heartening. Every incoming batch of prisoners told us of one victory after another. They assured us that the Krauts were fighting a losing battle and that the war would have to end soon. It couldn't be soon enough.

"Hang on, just hang on," Andy and I told each other, "it won't be long now." But we were both losing weight rapidly, and we were weakened by starvation and the intense slave labor, the deplorable conditions, even the nightly torture of the lice. Every night, I fell asleep with the subtle sound of hundreds of men crushing lice between their fingernails.

At the time, it seemed to me that nothing in my boyhood had prepared me for this experience, yet looking back, I realize that numerous things converged that helped me survive this critical challenge.

A buoyant personality had a lot to do with it. Early in life, I discovered that people like to laugh, and the class clown is often the most popular kid in school. I learned this quite by accident, actually.

While still in early grade school, my class was assigned to bring in a project about our hobbies. In fact, I did have an unusual collection. While working in Murph's, I came across a variety of tie pins among other old jewelry that my mother had bought from customers. From the 1800s through the 1930s, men wore a tie or stick pin in their dress ties as an important piece of personal jewelry. As Mother always encouraged us to broaden our knowledge with hobbies, she suggested that tie pins would make an unusual collection. I loved the idea and would spend a good deal of time organizing and categorizing my collection. My teacher chose a few children from the class, including me, to explain our hobbies to the class and to the parents on Parent's Day. This was more than I had bargained for. The whole thought of speaking in front of all those people filled me with dread.

I was as nervous as I could be as she called me to the front of the room to show my collection. The night before, I had been working at our store and had used an old rag to wash the glass showcases. A customer came into the store, and I began waiting on him. Unthinkingly, I stuffed the large, filthy rag into my pants pocket and forgot about it before going home. The next day when the teacher called on me, I went to the front of the room and nervously perused the audience. Sweating profusely, I reached for my handkerchief, but I pulled out the huge, dirty rag instead and proceeded to wipe my face with it. Instantaneously, laughter broke out all over the room. I looked down at the rag and did a double take in mock horror. More laughter! Even the teacher was wiping tears of hilarity from her eyes. I smiled amiably. Suddenly relaxed, I gave the funniest presentation the school had ever seen.

That night, as soon as Mom came home from work, she asked how my presentation turned out. I told her the story of the rag, acting out how I played up the comic scene. She exploded in shrieks of laughter, asking me to do it again. I don't remember Mom ever laughing so long and hard.

So I became the confirmed class clown—using humor to worm my way out of tight situations, seeing the funny side to every incident, and taking advantage of every opportunity to get a laugh. I admit that sometimes I went too far.

There was, of course, the unfortunate incident of the pig. I was only eight years old at the time, happily modeling clay in Miss Oxley's fourth-grade art class in Teller Elementary School. I decided to try my hand at creating an animal figure, and for some inexplicable reason I decided to form a pig. After some time and concentration, a beautiful pig emerged. I sat and stared at it, taking pride in the finished project. Then, a sly grin flashed across on my face. Was this a male or a female pig? In a wry quest for realism, I modeled the additional part, clearly determining its male gender. I had intended to remove the organ immediately after showing it to a couple of my friends. Predictably, they saw the pig and broke up with laughter. But I hadn't counted on the little girl in front of me turning around. The little prude caught a glimpse of my project and emitted a loud disapproving moan. Before I could correct my joke, Miss Oxley was standing behind me, twisting my ear. She confiscated the pig just as I had completed it.

I was sent home with a suspension letter stating that my mother and I were to appear the next morning in the principal's office. That night when my mother came home from work, I handed her the letter and explained what had happened. Yes, she was "disappointed," but there was no yelling or punishment. Instead, she took the opportunity to discuss why my joke was in bad taste. The next morning, when we entered the office of Mrs. Feltner, the principal, the pig was standing on her desk in all its anatomical glory. Mrs. Feltner swept into her office, trying to evoke a somber expression, but I detected a curled lip and a slight smile.

"An excellent rendition of a pig," she said.

"Yes, ma'am."

"Not nice, though. Do you know that?"

"Yes, ma'am."

"Why did you do it?"

"I wanted to make my friends laugh."

"And they did?"

"Um, yes. I was going to fix it afterwards, though. I wasn't going to leave it that way, honest!"

As a kind and wise educator, she accepted me back into the school and talked with me about the right way and the wrong way to use laughter. We all had a friendly, warm chat, and I developed a lasting admiration for Mrs. Feltner. I often wonder what ever happened to my pig.

Once in awhile I still used laughter the wrong way, and Mother would have to come down to the school and answer for my latest prank. But the confidence and personality I acquired were worth it. At least I thought so.

But nothing was funny at Gerolstein prison camp. The only time I heard my fellow prisoners exploding with mirth was when some poor guy fell into the huge latrine. The joke spread like wildfire through the entire building. We needed so desperately to laugh.

Though this was no place for jokes, my naturally droll state of mind had the power to uplift me and those around me, at least for a moment or two. Harking back to Mrs. Feltner's advice, this was the right way to use laughter. Use your talents for good, my inner voice told me; every quality can be used in the right way, if you try.

A strong sense of right and wrong had been inculcated in me throughout my life. Mother allowed us a lot of freedom, but she also had rules and was very strict sometimes. My brothers and I had responsibilities and learned to be accountable at an early age. Mother would let me know when I did something wrong, usually applying her lesson to the seat of my pants. The concrete values of hard work and self-sacrifice she taught me surfaced even before I went into the Army.

As a boy, I used to mow lawns to earn money. Our neighbors trusted me, and I always worked hard to do a good job. And like so many kids of that era, I was an "agent" for *Liberty* magazine, the *Saturday Evening Post*, and *Collier's Weekly*, selling subscriptions and delivering the magazines to my customers. Household money was scarce, but Mom made it clear that whatever money I earned was mine to keep. Talk about incentive!

One year, I had my eye on a new bicycle. I longed for that bike; I needed that bike, with the fancy chrome, the leather seat, and the shiny spokes. I decided to save up for it, stockpiling all my earnings for over a year to buy it. Finally, I had enough cash to buy my dream-on-wheels. But before I could go to downtown to make the purchase, I overheard something that gave me pause. Mother was telling a neighbor that she needed to put a new roof on the house, and that she might be forced to take out a loan to do it. She didn't want to take a loan: how in the world would she pay it back?

I decided to give all my hard-earned cash to Mother. She stared incredulously at my hand, extended toward her with my earnings.

"Ivan, where did you get all this money?"

"From my work in the summer and after school."

"But it's so much money."

"I've been saving it for a long time."

"And you're sure you want to give it to me—you're sure now?" She gave me a look that was at once poignant and skeptical.

"Yes!" I looked earnestly into her eyes. Mother never would have asked me for the money, but she was accepting gratefully. I knew I had done the right thing. As she gazed back at me, her face shone more than all the chrome bikes in Denver.

Looking back on it, I believe that the strength of character built throughout my childhood contributed to my maturity and ability to endure the hardships of prison life. I learned that there are times you just have to tough it out. With Mother's example, I learned never to feel sorry for myself.

Survival at Gerolstein was influenced by another factor, too: the power of memories. How desperately I wanted just to turn the clock back. And in my mind, I could do just that. Blessed with a strong imagination, I would revisit my boyhood and marvel at how good it had been.

As though pulled by a magnet, my thoughts would take me home to 815 Garfield Street, where I had lived my entire life. Though surrounded by the squalor of prison, in my mind I was taking the streetcar down Madison Avenue, getting off at the end of the line, and sprinting the few blocks to our little brick house. Bounding past the big old willow tree, up the stairs to the front porch, I'd open the door to our living room and then make my way to the kitchen at the back of the house.

The kitchen was where the real family action always took place. It didn't take much for me to envision Mother busily making jelly from the grapes she'd gotten from Uncle Harvey's grapevine across the picket fence next door. Or she'd be baking apple pies and strudel with apples from his tree. Even in Gerolstein, I could smell those pies.

I could picture our backyard, where I first heard Mother scream on that "date which will live in infamy."

It wasn't a big yard, but it had everything in it we ever would need. Mother grew her vegetables back there, and her beloved plants and flowers. Her favorite was lilacs, and in the spring, the delicate fragrance of Mom's flowers would suffuse our house. There was enough grass back there to play on, and room to kick a football—almost enough room. I could easily remember the time that I was practicing kicking field goals in the back yard. Mother's room faced the backyard, and she had put Max, who was an infant, in his bassinet there. My heart pounded as the ball crashed through the bedroom window. I raced inside, and there was Max, blissfully asleep, with broken glass all around him in the bassinet but not a scratch on him. I think it was then that I began to believe in miracles.

It would certainly take a miracle to get out of this disgusting, filthy, freezing prison camp, I reflected. I wondered what Max was doing now, at the age of fourteen. Was he practicing football kicks in the backyard? Was he thinking of his big brother, his soldier brother, who had disappeared?

Maybe he was practicing the jump shots I taught him at the basketball hoop behind the garage. Funny thing about the garage: We never had a car. When Mom and Dad bought the house back in 1922 (for the grand price of $2,500), the house came with that little garage in the corner of the yard. Maybe they dreamed that they'd own a car someday.

But Mother had made good use of the garage during the Great Depression, in her resourceful way. Our local barber, Mr. Young, had a car, and he asked Mom if he could rent the garage from her.

"I'll tell you what," she countered, "we can make a deal that's easier for you and better for me." He eyed her suspiciously. "You see those boys playing there, my boys?" She said, pointing. "Their hair grows faster than weeds. Suppose you give us free haircuts, and I'll let you use the garage." It was a deal. Throughout the Depression, we were best-groomed kids on the block.

And my mind inevitably zoomed back behind the garage to the alley, the gateway to all kinds of delights. Vegetable sellers, fruit peddlers, and the iceman would come down that alley. If you needed ice for your icebox, you put a card in the kitchen window, and he would stop in and deliver a block of ice. As he would go by, carefully carrying the block on his back, we kids would scramble for the ice chips, scooping them up, throwing them at each other, sucking them to get a refreshing cool drink on a hot summer's day. People who bought and sold rags, bottles, and all sorts of trinkets would come through the alley too. And then there was the popcorn truck. Each of these peddlers played his own special music: we'd hear them coming and run into the house to get a nickel, if Mom had one handy.

Dreaming of my boyhood while at Gerolstein was not always easy. Surrounded by disease and misery, with death hovering in the air as an ever-present phantom, Denver receded further and further from my conscious thoughts. With the stinking latrine and the hopeless expressions on my friends' faces, it was tough to remember a time and place when life was safe and normal.

Even the scarcest reminder of home was encouraging. Late one night, as we lay in the pitch-dark barrack, we were reminiscing about our favorite topic—food. A guy some distance from me said he used to work in a candy store next door to the Aladdin Theater. I perked up and shouted, "You said Aladdin Theater? Which one? Where are you from?"

"Denver!"

"Me too! My father used to take us to the Aladdin Theater on the streetcar. I used to go every week."

"I worked in the sweet shop next door."

"Wow! I don't believe it." I was smiling for the first time in weeks. I wanted so much to meet him, and I looked for him the next day. I never found him, but that voice in the night meant the world to me.

So I knew I had to at least try to counter depression, to keep in mind that that distant, comforting place called home not only existed, but still waited for my return. So I would tell Andy everything I could think of about my home and about my childhood, which now seemed remarkably quaint and lighthearted. My mind would meander through my memory, weaving one story into the next. Of all the places in that house, the most magical, I told him, was the front porch.

We used to play Monopoly there, and penny ball too. Jerry, Max, and I would put on shows on the porch as well, hanging up curtains around its perimeter, erecting a stage curtain, and setting up seats. The neighbors would pay five cents to watch the Goldstein Brothers perform skits and sing.

Music was a love we all shared. Mother would take us to summer band concerts in the park, and she infused our home with her own passion for music of all kinds. While she couldn't afford to buy musical instruments, one way or another, she saw to it that they made their way to us: we got a saxophone from my cousins and an upright piano from Mom's great-aunt. And somehow, she scraped up money or bartered for lessons. You'd walk into the house and hear Jerry practicing his scales on the sax and Max improvising on the piano. The most musical of all of us, Max also learned to play the sax, clarinet, and vibraphone (similar to a xylophone).

Probably the single most treasured item in our home was the phonograph player. I loved records, and those 78s yielded hours of inspiration, from the soaring notes of famous opera singers to the catchy ditties of Broadway musicals and popular songs of the 1920s and '30s. The powerful operatic voice of Enrico Caruso, that famous pioneer of recorded music, as well as Al Jolson, Fannie Brice, and Cantor Yossele Rosenblatt, could be heard playing, night and day.

I loved them all. I knew just about all of the songs by the Gershwin brothers, Irving Berlin, Jerome Kern—composers who shared my Jewish heritage and had evolved musically from the liturgy of Eastern European synagogues to the pop songs and swing of New York's Tin Pan Alley.

Opera and the classics were my favorites. As a teen, I shared this joy with my friend Eddie Bronstein, who loved opera too. Through him, I got a job as an usher at the Great Artist Series at the Denver Auditorium. The best musicians and singers played there. Ushers weren't paid, but I got to watch all the performances, and the best part of it was that I could go backstage to meet top performers. I got to see Gilbert & Sullivan musicals, watch incredible concerts, and meet the legendary violinists Yehudi Menuhin and Jascha Heifitz; opera greats Richard Tucker, Jan Peerce, Paul Robeson, Judith Anderson, and Roberta Peters; and pianists Arthur Rubinstein and Vladimir Horowitz. After seeing these greats of the musical stage, their recordings sounded even better to my ear.

The record player fed my humorous streak too. I would listen to old recorded comedy routines over and over, mouthing them along with the comic till I got them down pat. So our porch performances rolled together all of these influences—the humor and music we all knew from the radio and from our beloved record player.

I struggled to remember all the details of these times, to bask momentarily in the comfort of hometown warmth, even in the Hellhole of Germany. Huddled with Andy on the icy floor, I would tell him about warm summer nights when the neighborhood kids—Jewish, Italian, and

Irish—would gather on our porch. The porch swing would sway back and forth. We'd sit on the steps or lean against the house wall and gab well into the night.

It didn't matter that we were of different ethnic origins. Our strong sense of neighborhood overcame such divisions. Mother always said that the greatest blessing is to have good neighbors. And she was the epitome of a good neighbor herself, caring deeply about everyone and respecting each one's religious beliefs and observances, just as she received the same respect in return.

Next door to us was the Irish-Catholic Murphy family. A jovial, hard-working man, Mr. Murphy proudly worked for the Union Pacific Railroad. Perhaps recognizing that the fatherless boys next door may be lacking common things, he became like an uncle to us, giving us firecrackers in the summer and even taking us swimming with his family.

I liked Mr. Murphy, and I genuinely cared about him. Once, on my way home, I found him sprawled out on his porch. Was he dead? With tears in my eyes, I ran to the phone and called the police. They came and examined him, then smirked as they told me that he wasn't dead—only dead drunk. Did I catch it from Mrs. Murphy later that night! She bawled me out so much for calling the police that I never forgot it. So I learned to ignore Murphy's drinking binges. No matter how bad off he seemed, I would walk away, never again risking Mrs. Murphy's sharp tongue.

One of the fascinating things about Mr. Murphy was that he had fought heroically in World War I, and was one of the few survivors of the "Fighting 69th." Though not old, his hair was white. He swore it turned white overnight during a battle. We would sit on his porch and listen to his endless war stories. Most of the combat he had seen was hand-to-hand, fought in the trenches, and he described these in lurid detail. His favorite story was about the time he fought in a trench with a German soldier. He was out of ammunition, but he had a bayonet. The German was wearing a thick leather belt, but Murphy ran toward him at full speed and tore through the belt. "And that was the end of him," Murphy would conclude, slapping his thigh.

I would tell Andy Mr. Murphy's old war stories, but for the first time in my life, I realized that they might have been exaggerated. Were any of them actually true? It didn't really matter, we decided. What mattered is that he had survived to tell his tales. I would describe what a thrill it always was to see old Murphy strut in Denver's annual Memorial Day parade, holding his banner of the 69th high, and I'd imitate the old soldier's slow, prideful gait. It was good for our morale, good for a laugh. But when we stopped laughing, I wondered bitterly if I would ever march in that parade.

CHAPTER 8

The
Cattle Car

PNEUMONIA, MALNUTRITION, and frigid weather relentlessly stalked Gerolstein's inmates, and the death rate was accelerating. We all worried about catching some disease, for if a soldier came down with a fever, there was little chance of survival. But my greatest concern in the three weeks since I arrived there was about my feet. After the German soldier took my boots the day after I was captured, I had plodded for miles through snow and frozen mud, fighting sub-zero winds in only my socks and makeshift rag "shoes." My feet were wet most of the time, and now frostbite had numbed even the intense pain. Every night, I would remove the wet rags from my feet and replace the rags with dry ones. I noticed that my feet were turning dark in color, a sure sign of gangrene. For at least thirty to forty minutes every night, I would massage my feet, apprehensively trying to revive the blood circulation.

Though wave after wave of new prisoners assured us that the war was nearly over, incredibly, many more POWs were now coming to Gerolstein. Could our cramped, foul conditions be any worse?

Yes. There was now less space, less food, and more disease. "I can't survive this. I've got to get out of here," I reflected miserably. "Andy and I won't make it, it's impossible—unless something changes, and soon."

Then one day in mid-January, I heard an announcement that seemed to offer a chance of escape. "Achtung! If you are severely ill or wounded, report immediately to the doctor. If he determines that you are in serious danger, he will give you a ticket to be shipped out on tomorrow's train. Report now to the doctor."

I looked down at my swollen, blackened feet. Could they be my ticket out of the Hellhole? What about our pledge: could I get Andy out with me? And what about the rest of our foursome?

A plan began to percolate through my brain. But first, I needed a ticket. I limped to the doctor's office and showed him my feet. Holding my breath while he poked and prodded, I prayed that he would agree that I was one of the walking wounded ready to leave Gerolstein. Quickly, quietly, he handed me a ticket with "290" scrawled on it—my exit ticket. "You will give this to the guard at the train tomorrow night," he instructed summarily. "The lineup will be outside the barracks, next to the track."

That night, I showed the precious ticket to Urda, Kessler, and Lozano. They looked at it morosely and then quietly congratulated me on my good fortune.

"You don't get it, guys!" I cried. "We're all getting out of here with this!"

"But there's only one ticket," they retorted, practically in unison.

"I have a plan."

"Nothing can get us all out of here."

"We have to try, and we have to stay together. I'm willing to risk my ticket." They just shook their heads with negative resignation.

"Just listen to my plan." As they crowded around me, I whispered my idea. "The Germans move their trains only at night so they won't be spotted by the Allied air force. So it'll be dark. The four of us get on line—"

"Yeah, with one ticket. What's the use?"

"Hey, didn't you ever pass a basketball behind your back? When you were a kid, didn't you ever learn a sleight-of-hand magic trick?"

They stared at me in disbelief.

"Look," I continued, "we have to stand right next to each other, practically touching, with our hands behind our backs, like this." I passed the ticket quickly behind my back to Andy. "It'll just take a little coordination and practice," I urged. "I show the ticket and pass it to Urda, and Urda to Kessler, and Kessler to Lozano. With perfect timing and handwork, we all get on that train."

It was worth a try. The plan would work. It had to work. If it failed, we were all doomed to remain in Gerolstein and probably die there soon. We practiced over and over nearly all night, swiftly moving that piece of paper down the line till we had our technique down pat.

"What if the guard takes the ticket away from you, Ivan?" whispered Andy.

"Don't think about it."

Close to midnight the next night, the four of us stood next to the train, a line of cattle cars like the ones used for taking Jews to the concentration camps. Though these were smaller than American boxcars, the Germans were stuffing eighty men into each one.

We watched the guard carefully as man after man handed over his ticket and climbed aboard the train. It looked like the guard was handing the tickets back to them, but we couldn't be sure. We inched our way up the line, the four of us standing one against the other as we had practiced.

Finally, my turn came. Heart pounding, I swiftly flashed the ticket under the guard's nose and then handed it off to Andy. A split second later, someone shoved me into a boxcar and locked it behind me. I was number eighty in the first boxcar. I couldn't see out.

"Urda! Kessler! Lozano!" I wanted to shout, "Where are you?" But, of course, I swallowed the impulse, mutely straining to see between the slats into the darkness. It was nearly a miracle, I realized, that the guard didn't take my ticket from me. I had passed it successfully to Andy. What happened after that? Did they make it? Were they somewhere on this train, or had they been caught? Could they be executed for trying to outwit the guard? It was my idea. What have I done to them?

Andy! Where's Andy? Near panic set in when I realized I had lost my partner. Andy and I had grown truly dependent on one another. I wanted to cry like a child, feeling like I had been torn from my lifeline. I told myself over and over that my isolation was only temporary. He must be somewhere on this train. I'll find him when we reach our destination, and we'll have a good laugh. I've got to keep my sense of humor, I told myself. I've got to keep a calm perspective on this.

After an hour, the train began to move. As we kept saying during our captivity, "Nothing can be worse than this." At Gerolstein, we thought nothing could be worse. Wrong again! With eighty men packed in the car, I began to envy sardines in a can. At least they could lie down. I was lucky to get a space against one of the sidewalls of the boxcar so I could slide down and sit with my back supported by the wall. Metal drums were placed in the corners of the boxcar for toilets, but with the rampant dysentery among the passengers, they certainly were not sufficient. If you had to reach one of the drums from the center of the car, you were forced to climb over many people, and much of the time, the person failed to get to his destination in time. Some guys didn't even attempt to use the drums and relieved themselves where they stood. Adding to the animalistic stench was the fact that the cars previously had been used to ship cattle, and we stood on a floor covered with frozen manure. The only thing worse than standing on frozen manure was standing on manure that was defrosting because of all the people standing on it. This alone was enough for the facility to lose its five-star rating, I thought.

Somehow, I expected that we would arrive at our destination before morning, so I kept telling myself, "I just have to survive the next six hours." But from the small open spaces between the slats, I could see that we came to a stop while it was still dark. We remained stopped until daybreak. This was terrible news. As the Germans would move the train only by night, it undoubtedly meant that we would remain locked in the boxcars for another day. No one brought us food or water. No one came at all.

As daylight crept through tiny openings in the car, it became noticeable that icicles had formed on the ceiling and were dripping water. I watched as prisoners fought like animals to reach the ice. I hoped that I would never become that desperate. As for myself, I had saved part of my bread from last night's meal at Gerolstein and was looking forward to it as my morning breakfast. As I was munching on my bread, a frenzied prisoner tried to grab it out of my hand, but I managed to push him off and save it. I knew it was my last morsel until we would reach . . . wherever.

It dawned on me suddenly that maybe we walking wounded weren't headed for a German army hospital. Maybe they were disposing of us because we were too sick, because we were no longer of any use as slave labor. Many in the group were clearly very sick, and, in fact, during that day, two of the prisoners died. Their bodies were shoved to the end of the car, and everyone moved as far away from the corpses as possible. This made our luxury car even more cramped than before.

For the first time since we boarded, it was apparent that we might all die on this train. The extreme conditions, the lack of food, the questionable destination, and the ever-present stench of illness and death began to turn normal humans into animals. Crazed by suffering, all that was left was the animal instinct to survive. The voices that had started as quiet conversations when we left Gerolstein became louder and louder. Moans turned into soft sobs and then into loud wailing as the noise reached a crescendo of screaming and yelling. We were all going mad.

This episode was the worst I ever experienced. As I watched one man after another lose his sanity, I tried to block out what was happening around me by immersing myself in prayer. I focused constantly on God. "Save me, protect me, keep me safe," I muttered for hours on end. "Please don't let me lose my mind, just don't let me lose my

The single ticket the foursome—
Andy Urda, Ed Kessler, Ed Lozano,
and me—used to leave Gerolstein.

mind. . . ." I vowed that if God would deliver me from this terrible nightmare, I would never forget His constant presence in my life.

It was not unusual for me to turn to God at this moment of crisis. I had grown up with the story of how Mother had made her deal with her Divine Partner after Father died, and over the years, her staunch, enduring faith had become a part of me. Rocking to and fro, with the steady beat of the train wheels beneath my feet, my mind drifted to an incident that happened when I was about eight years old. My little brother Max was a baby of a year or two, and he was very sick, with a fever so high that the doctor said it could cause brain damage. Mother frantically tried everything to bring down his temperature, but nothing worked. Now she was panicking, screaming, crying uncontrollably as she rocked Max in her arms. I ran into my bedroom and prayed harder than I ever had in my life. "Please, please, save my little brother!" With my fists clenched and tears streaming from my eyes, I repeated my plea over and over. The fever broke that night. There was no question in my mind that God had heard my prayer and lovingly answered.

So I knew that He was listening, even in this stinking cattle car, with everyone around me going berserk. I knew He could keep me whole, keep me sane, if He wanted to—I just didn't know if He would. How long could I hold on? "Please, please, protect me. . . ."

We remained in the train for three full days, moving by night and stopped under cover of forests by day. Prisoners were dying one by one, and I continued my dialogue with God. On the third day, for some reason, our captors attempted to move during daylight hours. Allied fighter-bombers immediately spotted the train, and as a plane screamed by overhead—*wham*—a direct bomb hit on my car! The explosion was deafening, shrapnel flew in every direction, and bloody body parts streaked past me. The man on my right was cut almost in half; the head of the soldier on my left was cracked open.

I was untouched. Not a scratch. Quaking, I stood alone among the dead and critically wounded. It was truly a miracle.

I must have gone into shock, because I don't remember getting off the train or anything that happened immediately afterwards. The first memory I have, and I don't know how much time had passed, is that I was sitting in the snow among prisoners from the train. The Germans had given each soldier a can of meat and a piece of dark bread. Someone said that the can contained horse meat. Sickened by the thought of eating the stuff, I traded my meat with another soldier for his piece of bread.

I wondered if my friends had been on the train and if they had died or gone crazy like the others. With sad resignation, I concluded that I would have to survive without them, if I survived at all. Then someone kicked my foot. I looked up and staring down at me, gaunt but grinning, were Urda! Kessler! And Lozano!

I learned that my car was the only one bombed, and I couldn't figure out why. Almost sixty years later, Kessler told that me that some prisoners from the train had lain down in the snow and formed the letters *POW* with their bodies. The American pilots understood. There was no additional strafing, and the planes flew off.

In years to come, I blocked out this entire train experience, forcing myself to forget, for whenever I would recall these memories, they would make me sick. I allowed but one recollection to remain with me: my prayers had been answered. More, I had personally seen the powerful words of Psalm 91 come alive: "Thousands may fall at your side, but [harm] will not come near you . . . For he has yearned for Me and I will deliver him . . . He will call upon Me and I will answer him, I am with him in distress. . . ."

I would never forget my vow.

CHAPTER 9

Liberation

IN THE FOLLOWING DAYS, we were marched to a number of locations. *March* is not exactly the right word, for we dragged ourselves along, knowing that stragglers would be shot. Andy and I leaned on one another, trying to keep up a cheerful exchange that seemed more and more forced with every step. Kessler and Lozano shuffled along beside us. My recollection of the towns and villages we passed through are vague, for the suffering and shock blocked out a good deal. Most likely, I was only faintly aware of them at the time.

But I clearly remember reaching Stalag XII A in Limburg, Germany. (Stalag is the abbreviation of *stammlager,* meaning main camp.) The fact that this was a large, official POW camp raised our expectations: here, they would have to comply with international law, we reasoned.

There would be better food and facilities than at Gerolstein, and maybe even packages from the Red Cross. The Red Cross was known to send weekly packages of powdered milk, chocolate bars, cheese, and Spam to POWs.

One look at the prisoners in the camp crushed our optimism. Their faces were horrible, with sunken cheeks and haunted, lifeless expressions. Here too, starvation and hard labor had turned them into walking skeletons. And once again, our diet consisted of the same potato peel soup and dark bread, once a day. Sauerkraut was sometimes added, and to this day, I can't stand sauerkraut.

The only improvement was that we slept on straw, rather than directly on the ground. We knew that in a short time we would look like the rest of the inmates, if we didn't already.

Ever since my first and only interrogation, by the major who threatened to have me shot, no identification or names were asked. It was toward the end of the war, and the Germans were no longer keeping accurate records. We had all just become nameless slave laborers. But just in case, I hid my dog tags inside the rags covering my feet. I did not need it known that I was a Jew.

We didn't know then that the camp in Limburg was notorious for its terrible conditions. Its primary function was to act as a transit camp, the first point of interrogation and documenting of captured Allied prisoners. From there, they would be moved on to more organized and better-outfitted prison camps. So there never was any

Many who came in through the entrance of Stalag XII A never lived to go out of it. Here the gate is guarded by Allied troops after our liberation in March 1945 *Allan Jackson/ Keystone/Getty Images*

attempt to make conditions livable, even when a sizeable population of about twenty thousand wound up living there for long periods of time toward the end of the war. As usual, toilet facilities were grossly insufficient, medical aid was practically nonexistent, there was no heat despite the bitter cold, and the dismal place had no lighting. Night would come, and with it nearly total darkness. We would fall into our bunks like animals, dead tired from arduous labor. If the Red Cross was sending anything to Stalag XII A, we didn't know it.

Escape was unthinkable. We had been told in no uncertain terms that we would be shot if we so much as touched the tall barbed wire fence that surrounded the camp. We had no reason to doubt that the threat would be carried out.

Barbed wire also divided the camp into two sections: one housed American and British POWs. There was a good number of these, including soldiers from India serving in the British Commonwealth forces. They had been captured in North Africa in 1942, and I later learned that they were fairly well treated. The other side of the camp was for Russians. As in all German camps, the Russians were treated with particular ruthlessness, as though Hitler deliberately wanted to break down these sad remnants of Stalin's army. The Russians had a deep-seated hatred of their German captors. Their cities and villages had been destroyed; they had witnessed members of their families raped and murdered. And they swore that someday they would avenge the atrocities inflicted upon them.

We knew about the planned revenge, for Andy Urda's Slovak background enabled him to converse in a limited way with the Russian prisoners. With Andy as interpreter, we would talk through the barbed wire fence, exchanging news of the war on the Western and Eastern Fronts. The consensus on both sides was that the Germans were

Inside the barracks of Stalag XII A—a barn used for American prisoners. *The Granger Collection, New York*

retreating from both fronts and that it was just a matter of time until they would surrender. At least, we all wanted to believe that.

A break in the freezing weather also brought a rise in our spirits. What's more, several of our guards appeared to be only fifteen or sixteen years of age, a clear sign of dwindling German manpower. We taunted them that in less than a month their invincible German empire would be demolished. "Hey, why not set us free right now?" But they had been brainwashed to believe that this was not possible, and they swore that the Third Reich had recaptured Paris. England and America were next, they warned with glee. We didn't believe them. We held onto our hopes, bolstered by every new prisoner arrival, that the war was all but won.

Meanwhile, however, our daily slave labor would continue. We were divided into groups of ten prisoners, with one person responsible to deliver his unit's daily meal. I was in charge of my group and made out a list of the ten soldiers who depended upon me.

The one labor detail that never ceased was the burial detail. Unlike my previous experiences with this gruesome task, here the dog tags of the deceased were saved. We hoped they would be used for notification of their families.

At long last, the brutal winter was coming to an end. With the approach of spring, I experienced an indescribable, wonderful sensation that would repeat over and over through the years. During the previous months of captivity in sub-zero weather, my body never experienced a feeling of warmth. I was frozen to the bone nearly all of the time. When spring was in the air, I would go outside the barracks and sit in the brilliant sunshine, thirstily absorbing the sun's rays. The glorious feeling of heat penetrating my body was like a rejuvenating elixir. The sensation was beyond description, and to this day, whenever I sit in the sun, I recall that marvelous feeling.

Yet despite the renewal from the sun's warmth, I couldn't help noticing that my health was failing. The dysentery now was continuous; I was weak and dehydrated. My bones nearly protruded through my skin, and my face had taken on the hollow-eyed, sunken expression of the Limburg veterans. I could only pray that a liberating army would arrive before I became one of the victims of the burial detail.

Nevertheless, Andy and I continued our buddy system, sharing everything we had and trying to keep up the banter that would keep us sane. Then one day, Andy complained that his throat was so sore that he couldn't swallow. He had a fever and felt terrible. The health officer of the camp diagnosed diphtheria and sent him to an "infirmary" in the Russian section of the camp. This is the last time we'd see each other, I thought forlornly. After all we'd been through together, how could it end this way?

Within the next few days, I came down with the same symptoms. The health officer said that I also had diphtheria and ordered me quarantined to the Russian infirmary. I said goodbye to Lozano and Kessler.

I was taken to a one-room building measuring about twelve by fifteen feet. It was not an infirmary for treatment or care, but a means of keeping us from infecting other men with our sickness—a place to die. I looked around the room: there were eleven other men sprawled like mangled rag dolls on wooden bunk beds. Then I spotted Andy. He was still alive, I rejoiced, and we were together again. At least I wouldn't die alone.

Besides us, there were nine Russians and one other American. No one came with medicine, just a bit of food and water now and then. In the next few days, the nine Russians died and their bodies were removed. We three Americans were the only ones left in the room. Andy and I were too sick to move. I might have known the name of the other soldier at the time, but I was too ill to remember it afterward. I just recall that he was able to stand and walk around. Time ticked by slowly; night became day, and day turned into night. I don't know how much time passed.

Then one day the other soldier was peering out the window and started shouting with joy, "The Americans are here, the Americans are here!"

"Pipe down," I called weakly from my bed. "My head's spinning. What are you yelling about?"

"The Americans are here! It's over!"

"Can't be," I groaned. "Can't be true."

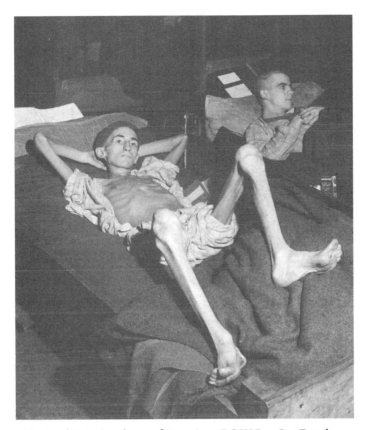

This April 1, 1945, photo of American POW Pvt. Joe Demler,
taken in Limburg after our liberation, shocked the readers of
Life magazine. Most of us—including myself—looked like him.
John Florea/Time & Life Picture/Getty Images

"But it is. I see them! Those are American tanks. I think it's the Ninth Army, and there's not a Kraut in sight."

We did not know that the camp had been evacuated. When the Allied soldiers began to cross the Rhine River in March 1945, German personnel began evacuating as many prisoners as possible. In one instance, 1,200 British and American prisoners in Limburg were packed into boxcars, bound for prison camps still under German control. Unmarked as POW trains, they were bombarded by U.S. planes, and many of the prisoners were killed. The Russian prisoners had been left behind along with the American prisoners too weak or sick to walk. My illness probably had prevented me from being put on that train. This was the third time I was saved from being killed by Allied bombers. This time, however, I wasn't even aware of it.

I don't remember the faces of the men who liberated us; don't recall the stretchers or the army doctors rescuing us from that chamber of death. I was too sick to notice anything. All I know is that the three of us were evacuated immediately to a nearby American field hospital. I was told afterwards by the doctors that if the camp liberation had taken place just a few hours later, they would not have found me alive.

They gave me a double injection of antitoxin serum for the diphtheria, figuring, I suppose, that the double dose might kill me, but the diphtheria surely would. As expected, I had a terrible reaction to the shot, but I lived through it and began to recover. I remember little else of the field hospital. Everything was a blur. Andy and the other guy seemed to be in better condition than I was. The three of us were taken to an army hospital in Belgium.

It was there that I insisted that a telegram be sent to my mother. "Please, just let her know that I'm alive. She's waited so long!" I knew that after all these months with no communication she would be overjoyed with the good news. I pictured her face when she would receive the telegram. She'd cry, yes, she'd probably cry. She'd run to show the telegram to Jerry and Max, and they'd hug and laugh; she'd race over to Uncle Harvey and to all the neighbors, waving the telegram and shouting with joy. And of course, she'd thank God. She always thanked God.

In fact, Mother did receive the much-awaited telegram, but the scene was not as I envisioned it. Someone mistakenly sent her a form telegram with the wrong message. Tearing open the envelope, Mother read, "Business is bad, need money immediately. Your son, Ivan."

Though mystified by the perplexing message, Mother was still ecstatic to receive anything signed, "Your son, Ivan." But she knew what to do. She contacted Colorado Senator Ed Johnson, who promised to find out immediately what the telegram meant. In a very short time, he called her back, excitedly telling her that the wording was a mistake, but the signature was true. "Ivan is alive," he exclaimed, "and recuperating in an army hospital in Paris!"

That was quite accurate. After my brief stay in Belgium, I was flown to Paris for further treatment. The trip was my first by air. I was amazed by the sensation of flight and buoyant in spirit as well. The nightmare was over. Though still sick and listless, I felt sure I would recover.

Andy and I parted in Belgium—a bittersweet moment, for he was going home at long last, and I would too, eventually. We knew neither of us would ever forget all we had been through together. Without trying, we could easily conjure images of months past: our capture beside the burning *Barracuda;* my near execution; our pact to become "one"; our sharing of every morsel of food; our intimate conversations through long, freezing nights; his escape from Gerolstein on my ticket; the bitter months in Limburg; and finally, that glorious, incomprehensible moment when we heard the shout, "It's over! The Americans are here!" There was really no need for promises to stay in touch. We shared one heart.

In Paris, my recovery was slow, but I gradually reentered the normal world—a world of haircuts, baths, shaving, and no lice. Eventually I was well enough to be taken in a wheelchair to see the sights. Hospital staff took us to the Eiffel Tower and to the wonderful museums. As an art student, I had often visited the Denver Art Museum and the Denver Public Library, so the most exciting excursions in Paris for me were to the Louvre and to the studio of Henri Matisse. The great artist was still alive at the time, and I got a tour of his studio, though I didn't see him. The art alone was enough to fill me with joy. What a thrill!

But I was reminded at every mealtime that I still had a long way to go before I would recover fully. I tried to eat regular food, but in my four months as a prisoner, my intestines had rotted, and I was unable to hold down food. I was placed on a special diet, the blandest stuff you can imagine, and little by little, there was progress.

Our ward was a long room with beds lined up on both sides. I noticed that some of them had red tags tied to them, and I thought that maybe these patients were receiving better treatment. I asked the nurse if I could have one of those special tags. *"Mais, non!"* She laughed, "No, you do not want such a flag!" She told me that the red tags indicated patients with advanced venereal disease, soldiers who had caught the disease from Parisian prostitutes. *"Non, non,* be glad you do not have that!" I chuckled at my own naiveté, realizing that not all of our ills had been inflicted by the enemy.

In addition to the sightseeing, the hospital tried to provide wholesome recreation. Periodically, a screen would be set up at the end of the ward and we were treated to popular movies. One day in April we were watching Judy Garland in *Meet Me in St. Louis,* when the movie was abruptly stopped. The lights went on, and there was a murmur of protest in the audience. Then came the somber announcement: "We regret to inform you that our president, Franklin Delano Roosevelt, has died." We were stunned.

Greatly loved and respected, President Roosevelt had sent us off to war to protect our nation and to save the world from a madman. We had tried to live up to the trust he placed in us. We had all seen our friends die on the battlefield, and we had been wounded in service to our country. The war was not yet over; how could he leave us now? I should add that at that point, most Jews were not aware that Roosevelt had obstructed plans to save Jews in Europe. Like all of our countrymen, we regarded him as a hero and the greatest American. He was genuinely mourned.

While in Paris, I received a letter from home informing me that—wonder of wonders—I was an uncle! Jerry's wife had given birth to a daughter. Overjoyed, I made a toy lamb for the baby from craft supplies the hospital gave the soldiers. The army had paid me my back salary from all those months in captivity, and I was feeling pretty flush. So, along with the lamb, I sent some perfume and other special gifts that I had bought.

From Paris, I was flown to a hospital in Glasgow, Scotland. I felt much better but was still battling to restore my stomach to a normal condition. As in France, I was taken on trips. Among other majestic places, I saw the famous Loch Lomond, twenty-four miles long and five miles wide. I remembered my father imitating Harry

Lauder, the Scottish singer who popularized this old song, among so many others: "Oh, ye'll tak' the high road and I'll tak' the low road/ And I'll be in Scotland afore ye . . . On the bonnie, bonnie banks o' Loch Lomond." Now, here I was, at this legendary place, humming that little tune, taking in all its beauty and wishing I had a sketch pad in my hand.

Yes, it's gorgeous, but it doesn't compare with our Rocky Mountains, I thought. It's not half as beautiful as Denver in the twilight. I yearned to go back—back to my hometown, to my brothers and cousins, my neighbors and friends, and, most of all, to Mother. It seemed like years since I had last seen them. Here I was, all of twenty years old, but I felt as if I had lived through a century. I felt aged and feeble. I had seen too much.

It did not take long before a number of patients were told we soon would be leaving for America. When? Tomorrow!

The next day found me dazed but joyous, waiting in line with other patients bound for the United States. Before getting on the plane, we were each weighed. It was worse than even I had imagined. At six feet three inches, my precombat weight had been 205 pounds. Now I was down to 96 pounds, and that was after being "built up" in the army hospitals. In those four miserable months, I had lost over half my normal weight. I was actually shocked, but my sense of humor was still intact. After they weighed me, I said, "Wait! That's not my true weight. I'm holding this paper—let me put it down." The guy behind me thought I was serious.

Accompanied by army doctors and nurses, we boarded the plane. The propellers whirred, and once again I was in the air, this time thankfully headed back to America. No words can do justice to the deep sense of gratitude I felt; no words can describe the intensity of my anticipation as we flew quickly, steadily home.

CHAPTER 10

Going Home

THE PLANE GLIDED SMOOTHLY onto the runway in New York, and we were taken to Mitchell Field Army Hospital. The doctors there told me that I needed an extensive period of recuperation and wanted to know if I preferred any particular army hospital. "Fitzsimons!" I told them jubilantly, "Fitzsimons, just outside of Denver."

It didn't take long for my choice to be confirmed. I was going home at last. I called my mother for the first time since going overseas.

After a few rings, she answered. "Hello?"

"Mom, it's me, Ivan."

She gave a loud scream of surprise and joy before shouting, "It's Ivan!" As we talked, I thought the sound of her voice was more beautiful than any music I had ever heard.

"Ivan, Ivan—how are you?"

"I feel fine, Mom." It was an outright lie, and she knew it.

"So you're coming home?"

"Well, not directly. I have to spend some time in Fitzsimons first."

"You're so fine that you're going to a hospital?"

"Well, I've lost some weight. They're going to build me up a little."

"Build you up better than your mother can? Tell them to send you home!"

"Not just yet, Mom. I'll call when I get to Denver tomorrow."

"Ivan, we can't wait to see you—Max, Jerry, everybody . . ." Her voice trailed off, choking with sobs. I knew the tears were of happiness and thanksgiving. Her Partner had answered her prayers.

We talked for a long while, and she gave me Uncle Nat Goldstein's phone number in Brooklyn, urging me to call without delay. I called Uncle Nat; he immediately phoned the head doctor of the hospital and told him he wanted to pick me up and drive me to Brooklyn for a family reunion. He guaranteed that I would be back at the hospital in the morning. Hearing the urgency in Uncle Nat's voice and the details of my story, the doctor kindly approved an overnight pass for me.

Uncle Nat picked me up at the hospital, and soon I was shuffling into Aunt Sara's house amid joyous cries of "Ivan's here!" The entire New York Goldstein clan, aunts, uncles, and cousins—all the same people who had seen me off before I shipped out—were together again at Aunt Sara's. Could it have been only seven months since the last time I had heard "Ivan's here"? The change in me must have been terrifying to them. In place of the robust young soldier confidently going off to war, they saw an emaciated creature of skin and bones, aged by experiences they didn't dare to imagine. Though I tried to smile bravely, they could see that I didn't feel well at all.

They told me my Great Aunt Leah from Denver, the widow of my beloved Uncle Block, was visiting his family in New York and would be coming over to see me. I was anxious to see her too. Much of the spiritual strength I absorbed as a child was provided by the richness of her traditional Jewish home; it had sustained me through my recent trials. She strode in, glowing and happy, but the smile on her face froze when she saw me. I gave her a reassuring grin, but the tears in her eyes told me everything. No doubt, she would call my mother to prepare her for the sight. Maybe it's better that way, I reflected.

Our reunion was wonderful, though now and then someone would look at me and begin to weep. "Hey, I'm fine. Really, I'm in great shape now," I laughed. "You should have seen me before!" I guess the contrast with my previous visit was overwhelming.

Surrounded by family, my mind skipped to earlier trips to New York—particularly with my father when I was only about five years old. The oddest recollection came to mind. I pictured myself in the basement of Zaidy Goldstein's house. This was where he made his own cherry wine, and he was showing Jerry, my cousins, and me his collection. "I'll give you each a taste," he teased, "and the one who asks me the nicest will get the bigger glass." Jerry went first, smiling adorably and saying, "please." Each of my cousins implored sweetly, but I won, hands down, with "Zaidy, dear, may I please have a glass of your wonderful wine?" Even at five, I knew the score.

At Zaidy's house, I also sipped a memorable soda pop—Dr. Brown's Celery Tonic. I never forgot that taste. What sweet little memories! But this time, fifteen years later, my evening with the Goldsteins was on a more somber note. Reluctantly, but with an intense desire to share my pain, they asked me about my war experiences and listened in stunned silence past midnight. When it was over, I was exhausted and they were crying.

Aunt Sara woke me for breakfast. I had to get back to Mitchell Field for my flight to Denver in the afternoon. Uncle Nat was running late when he came to pick me up. We scrambled into the car, and he floored the gas pedal. Streaking down the highway at top speed, he saw in his rear-view mirror that a highway patrolman was in hot pursuit. The cop pulled him over, admonished him for speeding, and wrote out a hefty ticket. Uncle Nat briefly told him I had been a POW, stressing that he was rushing only because he had to get me back to Mitchell Field for my flight home. "Oh, yeah?" the officer snarled. He peered into the car and looked me in the eye. His features softened, and he turned away. Then, tearing up the ticket, he thanked me for my service to our country and waved us on.

My flight arrived at Buckley Air Force Base outside of Denver in the evening, and an ambulance waited there to take me to Fitzsimons hospital. It was well after nine o'clock by the time I was checked in and assigned to a bed and, to tell the truth, I needed to sleep. As much as I wanted to see my family, it was too late for a reunion with them. I called Mother, and it was decided that they would come to the hospital in the morning. I gave her directions on how to find my building inside the Fitzsimons complex. "You probably won't recognize me," I remarked affably, "so I'll be outside on the grass with a pink carnation pinned to my pajamas."

We both knew that it wasn't much of a joke. It had been almost a year since my mother had seen me, and now meeting her son as a hundred-pound skeleton would be quite a shock. It would be an even bigger jolt because I had been sending her reassuring letters from the hospitals in Europe, downplaying my true condition, only casually adding that I had "lost a little weight." I meant what I said about meeting them outside. I didn't want our emotional reunion taking place inside the ward.

It was a beautiful, sunny day in May. I was out there early, waiting impatiently when they drove up. In the car were my mother, two brothers, sister-in-law, and Joe Hirsh, a distant cousin of Mother's. Joe repaired watches for Murph's customers, and he proved to be a truly caring relative. Since the moment I was reported missing in action, he had been in continual contact with Mother and Jerry, trying in numerous ways to bolster their hopes. He repeatedly told them that he was convinced that I was alive and would be coming home. "I want to be there," he'd say, "I want to be there when Ivan comes home, so don't forget to call me."

The car door opened, and there was Mother rushing toward me, her arms outstretched. I remember throwing my arms around her and holding her close for the longest time. I couldn't let go. All the tears that I held back during my captivity now ran freely and trickled onto her hair, her forehead, her cheeks. During the long embrace, Mother held me very close, very tight, her eyes closed, but there were no tears. It could be that she had cried for so many months that now she had no tears left, only thanksgiving. But my brothers were crying.

Or could it be that she was, once again, setting an example for her child? Through the years, she often had exhibited stoic qualities, pushing onward to better our lives through sheer determination. Though she panicked inside when her children were endangered, she would take care not to frighten us but to act as calmly and decisively as she could. She had weathered cuts, bruises, and broken bones.

Of course, once the crisis was over, she would store these incidents in her mother's bag of complaints. Every so often, she would wryly remind us of all she had gone through with Jerry and Max. At these moments, I would triumphantly say, "But Mom, from me you never had trouble!" Until now, that is. She had suffered the trauma of the telegram telling her I was missing, the long months of waiting, watching for news, latching onto any sign of hope. And now she stood there, staring at the wan face of her son—her previously healthy, athletic boy—with his pajamas hanging from his shoulders like oversized rags around a pole. She took it all in and swayed a bit, as though she were about to faint.

"At least he's alive, Ida," Joe whispered. "He's alive. That's all that matters."

To tell the truth, when I saw Mother I was shocked too. There were lines on her face that had never been there before. Her eyes seemed softer and deeper, and her brow was more wrinkled than I remembered. The energy she had expended fighting off dark thoughts and fears had left her weary and spent. I knew that enduring the trial of my uncertain fate as only a mother can, her strong faith had prevailed. And yet, I could see that she would never be quite the same again.

Once she saw me, Mother understood why I could not yet come home. In fact, the damage to my gastrointestinal system was so profound that I needed nine months at Fitzsimons hospital to heal. Moreover, my teeth had suffered a good deal too, and the dentist had his work cut out for him. There were occasional passes granted to go home, but even after discharge, I had to keep coming back to the hospital for treatments.

My stay in the hospital was more pleasant than I thought it would be. When the war in Europe was over on May 8, 1945, my fellow patients and I shared the joy of reading the top news stories. The *Denver Post* headline screamed, "TRUMAN AND CHURCHILL PROCLAIM COMPLETE VICTORY OVER GERMANY," and the front-page stories assured us, "GERMAN ARMY CHIEF PLEADED FOR MERCY AT PEACE SIGNING," followed by, "BODY OF HITLER FOUND, RUSSIAN GENERAL CLAIMS." A banner headline in the *Rocky Mountain News* rejoiced, "This Is V-E Day," and announced, "TRUMAN ON AIR 7 A.M. TODAY."

Visits from my family were frequent, and Max (fourteen years old at this point) was especially devoted. He would come and watch movies with me. Army buddies who had concluded their service in Europe or were on furlough came to see me. I learned that after I was taken captive, the 11th Armored Division had fought on in the area west of Bastogne but suffered significant losses. Over the next few days, they took Lavaselle and the village of Chenogne, sometimes with hand-to-hand combat, and pushed on a day or two later to take Mande Saint-Etienne. Around the time that I was dodging Allied bombers on the railroad tracks near Prüm, they were resting in the village of Berchcux. There, they whitewashed the tanks so they would be less of a target in the swirling snow. I thought this was a clever idea, and I wished we had thought of this camouflage before that fateful day of destruction for the *Barracuda*.

Their battles continued north of Bastogne during the arctic weather of mid-January. As I shivered in Gerolstein, they were fighting frostbite in their tanks. There is no place colder than a tank in freezing temperatures. Rather than shield its crew from the cold, frost forms on the metal interior, in effect turning the entire tank into a huge icebox. Many a soldier was sent to the medics with frozen feet. The tank drivers had trouble maneuvering in the icy conditions too, as freezing rain caused them to slide uncontrollably. In fierce fighting, they had lost one commander after the other, fighting almost each new day under an acting commander, some of whom had little or no leadership experience.

They moved steadily toward the Siegfried Line, the long barrier Germany had constructed along its western border as a foolproof line of defense. They crossed the Our River, and though neither they nor I knew it, they were right on my heels, following the route I had taken just weeks before. As I was being moved about in Germany, the 11th Armored followed: they passed through Prüm and Gerolstein and later turned southward. On March 29, the day that I was liberated from Stalag XII A, they were crossing the Rhine River on pontoon bridges near the city of Oppenheim. They pushed on through desperate battles deeper and deeper into central Germany. And they were shocked to the core when they saw Mauthausen Concentration Camp, where the gas chambers and crematoria were still in operation when they arrived. What they saw in the camps was so heartrending that even soldiers toughened by bloody battles and harsh conditions could not even talk about it.

We shared news of what happened to our friends, and I discovered that a good number of people were headed back to the war after their brief stay in the United States. The army had set up a point system for discharging soldiers coming back from Germany. It was based on military service, time overseas, and time in combat. Many of the soldiers coming back from the war in Europe didn't have enough points for discharge and were sent to the Pacific conflict.

One of the most painful meetings I had was with the father of my tank commander, Staff Sgt. Wallace Alexander. The last time I saw him on the day of our capture, he was screaming in agony as the Germans carried him off. I assumed that his wounds were critical. His family, however, was never notified of his whereabouts. When the war in Europe ended, Wally's father tracked me down and came from his home in San Francisco to Fitzsimons hospital. He knew I had been in the same tank with Wally, and he came hoping I could give him some assurance that his son had, in fact, made it through the war.

A distinguished looking gentleman, Mr. Alexander said he felt that Wally was alive—that he must be somewhere in Europe. I'll never forget the tears trickling down the old man's face as I told him that his son had been wounded, very badly wounded in both legs, and how we had tried to help him. I suggested quietly that if he hadn't heard from Wally by now, it might be better to assume the worst.

But old Mr. Alexander wouldn't give up. He went to Europe to find his boy. I was told later that he located the spot where the tank had been destroyed and traced Wally's journey. He found out about the German military hospital and he talked to everyone he could find who had been there, who may have worked there, anyone who might remember the American soldier Wallace Alexander with severe leg wounds.

His perseverance paid off. Somehow, he found the medic who had attended Wally. The German medic clearly remembered that they had amputated the sergeant's leg, but the wounds had been too profound for him to survive. He was there when Wally died, and he had personally buried him. The medic assured the grieving father that he had left Wally's dog tags on him so the body could easily be identified—and then he took him to the grave. That was the end of the search. I was

Wallace Alexander's grave.

not there at that tender moment, but I can imagine his reaction when he saw the grave. Mr. Alexander understood that he would never again see his son alive, but at last he had found him, and that was some consolation. He brought Wally's body back to San Francisco, where it was buried with full military honors.

But it was counterproductive for me to dwell on the horrors I had seen. I needed to get back to my old self, back to a youthful, happy outlook. The ward began to fill with returning GIs, and a strong feeling of camaraderie developed among us. Some of them, suffering from serious ailments, were fairly glum. They need to be cheered up, I thought. One day, a crazy idea came to me, and I prepared my friends for what I was about to do.

Because I was taking sulfa medication that could be damaging, daily urine testing was a must. As usual, the nurse had brought me a clear plastic container for my urine sample. I took a glass of apple juice from my breakfast tray and poured it into the container. When the nurse came to pick up the urine sample, she commented, "It's a little cloudy this morning."

"Let me see," I said, taking the container from her. "You're right! Well, let's just run it through again and maybe the second time it will look better!" Then I quickly drank the entire contents. Her mouth fell open in horror. But the loud bursts of laughter from the other patients made her realize the wild joke. Ivan the prankster was at it again. And boy, did it feel good!

At Fitzsimons, I was introduced to a sport that was to become a lifelong hobby. One of my doctors felt that I could recover from my weakened condition by walking every day, and he asked me if I had ever played golf. Aside from hitting balls on a driving range now and then as a youngster, I had never played the game.

"Fine," he smiled. "We have a nine-hole course here on the hospital grounds and clubs available for patient use. You can buy balls in the pro shop."

It sounded like a great idea. I had always liked sports, so I started playing nine holes several times a week. I might add that although I had tried most sports in my youth, after my four months of frostbitten misery in Germany, I could never take up winter snow sports, such as skiing or iceskating. I had seen enough snow to last a lifetime.

But golf—now that's another matter. Give me a nice, breezy day, with the sun beating down, warming my skin, and I will be out there with my clubs. It's a great sport. But back at Fitzsimons, even this innocent pastime evoked "war nerves" when I least expected it.

Ironically, recovering U.S. soldiers shared this army hospital with a good-sized contingent of German POWs who had been assigned there to work in the laundry, the mess halls, and gardening—what a difference from the way we were treated. One of the first times that I played golf, I faintly heard the familiar guttural sounds of the German language being spoken nearby. At first, I thought that my mind was playing a devilish trick on me, that I was hearing things, but then I realized that it was only the German prisoners detailed to golf-course maintenance.

I hit my drive to the right side of the fairway. Walking toward the spot where the ball should have been, I saw there was no ball. A German worker was standing there. I asked him if he had seen the ball; he shook his head no and kept working. I knew he must have picked up my ball, but I had no proof. A few holes later, I hit a ball into the rough. The Germans there said they didn't see it, but anxiously added "We'll sell you some." They showed me a bag with about twenty golf balls, the thieves!

"I'll take 'em all," I said, grabbing the bag. I started to walk away.

"Where's the money?" they demanded.

"There is none!" I answered, and the chase was on. They came after me, yelling that they wanted their money. Suddenly I turned, grabbed a golf club, and swung it wildly. "You come near me, and I'll kill you with this club!" I must have looked like I meant it. They stopped, but continued screaming. "Just one step closer and I'll kill you!" I threatened. They retreated, cursing me in German. It took me a while to stop shaking.

At the pro shop, I reported what had happened, and they said that similar complaints had been made, and that they would handle the situation. I heard some days later that the entire group of German prisoners had gone on strike because they were being served meat "only" a few times a week. I was furious.

As I was a returned prisoner of war, military investigators came to the hospital to hear the complete story of my captivity. I vividly recalled the incidents I had witnessed of German soldiers killing Americans and told them approximate times, locations, and circumstances of the events. One of the events of an American soldier being murdered had been reported in almost identical detail with my information. I also remembered a particular American prisoner who had become a *kapo*, essentially a turncoat who would assist the Germans in return for special privileges. In this case, he was relaying information he heard from prisoners that would be of use to the German army. For his help, the Germans gave him special quarters and food. He would trade the American prisoners extra food for cigarettes or for their hidden jewelry or money. I remembered the American's name. The man taking down my testimony told me there had been other complaints about the same soldier. He thought my testimony would be of great help in tracking down the guilty individuals.

After hearing my entire story, the officer asked to see my two wounds, the one from the bullet that had pierced my leg when I ran along the top of my tank and the other from shrapnel at the train tracks. I felt this request was very odd but showed him. Gaping at the scars, he announced, "You're entitled to a Purple Heart!"

About a week later, I was stunned when a major came to the ward looking for me. After a brief ceremony, he presented me with not one, but two Purple Heart medals "for wounds received in action against the enemy."

But there were also scars that couldn't be seen. The human mind is an extraordinary thing. It not only stock- piles information, it is adept in storing terror. Beneath the layers of conscious recovery, emotional memories of unbearable magnitude lurked unseen.

As it happened, Fitzsimons hospital was in line with three airfield flight patterns. At night, while I was sleeping, the sound of airplanes unleashed nightmares that would wake me up tossing in a cold sweat and screaming—reliving the horror of hearing the whir of bombers overhead as we scrambled for cover. (These nightmares continued into the first years of my marriage, when I would wake up screaming

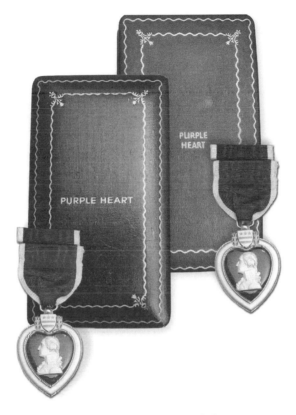

The two Purple Hearts I received while recuperating
at Fitzsimons Army Hospital.

and swinging as though to protect myself. Over the years, I
thought I had left them behind but was eventually shocked
to discover that at the most profound level, they were still
with me. Deeply sedated in a recovery room after surgery
just a few years ago, I started yelling "Watch out, Andy,

look out!" The dark specter of peril that I thought I had buried sixty years before had suddenly reemerged.)

The goal during my time at Fitzsimons was, of course, to forget my ordeal and enjoy the loving support of my family and friends who now surrounded me. As I was getting stronger, I was allowed overnight passes home twice a week. On one of these occasions, my mother threw an open-house party, inviting all the neighbors on the block. In those days, people didn't move to new homes as often as they do now: many people lived in one house most of their wedded life. So for the most part, on my return, the neighbors were the same I had known all my life. When word had gotten out that I was missing in action, they had sincerely worried about me, doing all they could to shore up Mother's spirits. When Mother invited them to our party, they were overjoyed. I walked in, and there they were—the Murphys, the Urpshausers, the Gabels, the Pecks, the Ziskas, the Boslows, the Greinetz family, of course, and every neighbor I had ever known, with smiles on their faces and tears in their eyes. I was never hugged and cried over so much in my entire life.

And one of the best benefits of coming home was getting every kid's dream at Walter's Drug Store. In those days, a drug store was not just a pharmacy. Many of them also had a soda fountain where they served all sorts of refreshments. This was the place we had always gone to get ice cream cones, five cents for a double-decker, or an ice cream soda—with two scoops—for ten cents. My favorite was Walter's terrific Cherry Submarine—soda, ice cream, cherries, whipped cream, and nuts. My mouth still waters just thinking about it.

What does a starving prisoner of war think about? In my case, Cherry Submarines were at the top of the list. Sometimes I could picture old Walter behind the counter, squirting layer upon layer of whipped cream over that ice cream, and the thought alone would give me pleasure. From my European hospital bed, I once wrote home that in the POW camp I dreamed about Cherry Subs. I soon got a letter with a coupon enclosed. It read, "This entitles the bearer to 20 free Cherry Submarines at Walter's."

Needless to say, I used up that coupon pretty quickly when I came home. When I turned it in for the twentieth time, I lamented aloud that I was eating my last free sub. Walter came over to where I was sitting, gently placed his hand on mine, and said "Son, it's a lifetime offer."

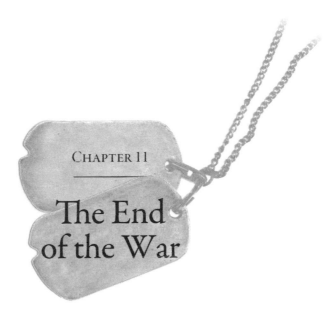

CHAPTER 11

The End of the War

PATRIOTISM RAN HIGH, and everyone knew that the end of the war was near. This feeling became more intense when soldiers started coming back to the United States from the battlefronts and prisoner of war camps. Every city and town across America feted its returning GIs. We were treated royally everywhere. We could travel on buses and go to movies and shows for free. We were invited to parties, and we visited celebrities at the Stage Door Canteen. At the Stage Door, I watched a rising young singer perform. His name was Frank Sinatra. He was pretty good, I thought.

The spirit that animated our lives then was powered by the fact that everyone—military or civilian—participated in the war effort. Unlike today, where only the soldiers and their families directly feel the effects of war, Americans in the 1940s backed the war wholeheartedly and were called upon to make sacrifices for it. They were invested in it emotionally, morally, and financially.

I had been in Fitzsimons for over three months now, and my progress was visible. I was gaining strength, putting on weight, and the sparkle that had once been in my eyes was returning more often. I could come and go from the hospital, as long as I was there for treatments, tests, and to take my medicine.

An old school friend, Leonard Strear, came home from his service in Europe and visited me at Fitzsimons. Leonard had a car, so he would pick me up at the hospital for short jaunts and bring me back. One day in August, he suggested that I get a three-day pass from the hospital so we could take some road trips to the majestic Colorado Rockies and spend some restful hours there. I got the pass, and we headed for Estes Park, a scenic spot adjacent to Rocky Mountain National Park. We rented a mountain cabin and stretched out to relax, listening to music on the radio.

Leonard had brought a bottle of Southern Comfort liquor and was mixing it with Coca Cola. Because of my sensitive stomach, I couldn't drink spirits; I was more than content to simply enjoy the classical music humming on the radio. He was on his third or fourth drink when the music stopped playing, and an excited voice cried, "We interrupt this program for an important announcement: The Japanese have surrendered!"

It was August 14, 1945, the day that came to be known forever after as VJ Day, the day all America went wild. Victory over Japan meant that the war was over. Giddy with joy, Leonard and I agreed that we must get back to Denver immediately. Ten minutes later, we were hurtling down the winding mountain roads. I saw right away that Leonard couldn't handle the twisting road. We tore faster and faster around curve after curve, our wheels narrowly missing the edge. The trees became a blur.

I can't believe this, I was thinking. I can't believe that I made it through combat and freezing winds and slave labor and POW camps just to wind up shooting off a mountain into a canyon!

"Len, you've got to slow down! Listen, let's stop at Grand Lake. You know my crazy stomach. I need some food and a restroom. OK? Let's stop there for a couple of minutes."

We came to a stop in the parking lot of the Grand Lake Restaurant. I felt like I'd have to peel my fingers off the dashboard one by one. I dawdled and delayed at the rest stop, urging him to have something to eat (and how about some nice, strong coffee?) and stalled some more. When I was sure he was better, we continued our trip. Some hours later, he dropped me off at home and he said he'd pick me up in thirty minutes to go downtown.

When we got there, the whole town was celebrating. After four grueling and bitter years of death and sorrow, the war was finally over. It was a euphoric scene—everyone was kissing, and people were on top of buses and cars—crowds literally dancing in the streets. I suppose every city in America was like that. Those of us who had been overseas—and there were many of us—danced with joyous abandon, thankful that our nightmare was over, that no more men would be sent over to kill or be killed, and that all we had fought for was finally achieved.

Leonard and I stayed till well after midnight. That night, I went home instead of back to Fitzsimons. I wanted to be where I had been when the Japanese had bombed Pearl Harbor nearly four years before.

The end of the war made me anxious to get out of Fitzsimons and get on with my civilian life, but my doctors insisted that I remain because my health problems were not fully cured and I needed further treatment. I had planned to reenter the University of Denver (DU) on the GI Bill to finish my education. I chose this college because I did not want to leave Denver. I had traveled far enough and been separated too long from my family to even think of leaving again.

I missed registration for the fall semester, but in December, I convinced the doctors that I could continue outpatient treatment at the veterans' hospital, and they agreed. I was discharged from the army and from the hospital. My stint with Uncle Sam was finally over.

I registered for the winter quarter at DU with a fine arts and commercial art major. Before my education had been interrupted by the war, I had joined a Jewish fraternity, Phi Sigma Delta, Chapter IOTA. By 1943, the chapter had become inactive because there were so few men left at the university.

When I returned to college, alumni from the University of Denver and the University of Colorado contacted me and asked if I would take on the task of reactivating the Jewish fraternity at DU. I agreed to do it. It was my first volunteer job in community-related work, and it set a precedent that lasted throughout my life.

The alumni offered to send me to the National Fraternity Convention at the Waldorf Astoria Hotel in New York. There, I would meet with national officers and get the backup support I needed to restart the DU chapter. Great! I'm ready to go, I told them, and almost instantly regretted it. I had no civilian clothing. I was still in my army uniform, and the last thing I wanted was for people to ask me about my war experience.

But I couldn't just go out and buy new clothes. Back in 1945, clothing manufacturers had been working under military contracts, producing uniforms. Some were in the process of converting their operation back to designing and manufacturing civilian clothing, but there were few who had made the change. It was nearly impossible to buy a man's suit at that time, if indeed you could afford one.

But I decided that the trip to New York was a chance I shouldn't miss, so I took the train and, once again, made my entrance at the Goldsteins of Brooklyn. As always, they were cordial and welcoming—and this time they were overjoyed that I had arrived in time to attend my Uncle Phil's wedding. I told them I had come for the convention, and even mentioned how uncomfortable I was to still be in uniform. "Call Etta! Call Etta!" someone urged, and before I knew it, my Aunt Etta was on the line.

A true Goldstein, Etta was entranced with the world of music, and she had once aspired to be an opera singer. She quickly discovered that her dream would never come true, and she opted for a more practical route. She went to work in a dress shop owned by a Mrs. Alexander and eventually became highly successful in the clothing business. In other words, she had connections in the clothing industry that were firmly closed to outsiders. (Etta became a buyer for a big chain store and ultimately transformed herself into a woman executive in an era when there were very few. I surmise that the name Goldstein was an impediment to her career, however, because she used the name Olsta instead.)

Etta showed up the next day and surveyed me thoughtfully. "No, no, this will never do. Ivan, we've got to get you a new wardrobe!" She whisked me off to a wholesale clothing manufacturer, and I spent the morning climbing in and out of one suit after another. By noon, she had bought me two suits, a sport coat, and a pair of slacks. Not only did I have suits to wear at the convention, I was the best-dressed guy in Denver for years.

I had been warned not to mention the war to Etta. The rumor was that before World War I, she had been engaged to marry a fellow who went into the navy and was sent overseas. He never came back. Over the next few years, I learned that there were many like her as a result of both World Wars. Not only were there "war widows" whose husbands died in the service, there were thousands of young women like Etta, hopeful brides who never again saw their beloved alive. So we had a silent understanding not to mention the war, for both of our sakes.

Aunt Etta and I focused on the task at hand. The rest of my family joined in too. It was as though, this time, they were determined to put my war ordeal behind me and make my vacation with them as carefree and fun-filled as possible. It was a wonderful week of sightseeing and shows with the cousins, aunts, and uncles. I then returned home to start the rest of my life.

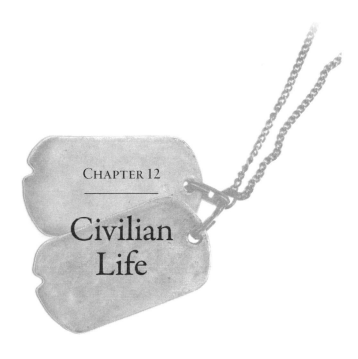

CHAPTER 12

Civilian Life

IMMEDIATELY WENT TO WORK on the reactivation of the Phi Sigma Delta fraternity. Before the war, our membership was made up almost entirely of Denver residents, but now returning GIs wanted to settle in Colorado, and we opened our doors with twenty new members, many from out of state. The frat became a vital source of social, sports, and religious activity for Jewish male students.

My mother always encouraged me to choose my friends carefully. Be close to good people, she urged, people from whom you can learn something. If she disapproved of a friend, she would discourage the association. A perceptive judge of character, she would base her opinion on her observations of the family as well as the person. In general, I listened to her, and she usually liked my friends. On a few occasions, I disagreed with her about someone. Looking back on it, she was always right. Moreover, she taught us—through word and example—that you should hold on to people who are good friends, stick with them, and I did. My friendships brought me great joy and fulfillment over the years.

One such friend was Dave Spivak. His grandfather was the renowned Dr. Charles D. Spivak, who headed a tuberculosis hospital just outside Denver. Founded in 1904, his Jewish Consumptive Relief Society became world famous. (The Denver climate is very beneficial for lung problems, and there are still numerous renowned hospitals there for treating lung-related diseases.) Dave's father, H. David Spivak, was a famous painter, known especially for his landscapes and portraits.

Dave and I were inseparable during our school years, for we had much in common. We both lost our fathers at a young age. Raised by our working mothers, we were taught to work hard, do well in school, and appreciate the arts. Unlike me, however, Dave didn't have much of a connection with Judaism and didn't even plan to have a Bar Mitzvah. His indifference bothered me. When he claimed that he did not know the necessary blessings and rituals, I quickly volunteered to work with him. I did, in fact, teach him the blessings and *haftorah*, the biblical passages chanted aloud in Hebrew, expected of a Bar Mitzvah boy

Dave Spivak and me: friendship reunited
after I left the army, 1946.

at that time. It was a proud day for me when I attended his
Bar Mitzvah.

But in high school, Dave's talent as an athlete led him
to other social groups, and our friendship seemed to fade.
During the war, he also was in the ASTP and wound
up going overseas. He came home from Europe in fine
shape. We picked up as close friends again, as though
nothing had ever separated us. A superb athlete, Dave
loved handball, racquetball, softball, and golf. We were
inseparable again.

Now that we were both at DU, Dave joined my fraternity. In fact, Dave and two other members became that
"old gang of mine." We spent most of our time together

on campus, on summer vacations, and on Saturday nights. Dating, sports, even weekly pinochle games revolved around the gang.

Dave and I would remain great friends throughout our lives, our friendship deepening and growing. We both got married around the same time. We both had four children, and our families enjoyed spending time together. Later in life, he visited my new home in Jerusalem, and whenever I came back to Denver for a visit, I'd make it a point to see him—often, several times a week, just like in the old days. He always pushed himself as an athlete, playing softball and volleyball, even when he was elderly and had a heart condition. The day he died, he had just played a few games. He was seventy-five. I was in Israel at the time and couldn't come to the funeral, but I sent the speech I would have made, and my son read it aloud at the funeral. Now, whenever I go back to Denver, there is an empty feeling, hard to describe. "Where's Dave? He should be here." My mind knows he is not there, but my heart does not. You don't have that type of friend more than once in a lifetime.

But during our college days, with so much of our lives ahead of us, Dave and I simply shared all the excitement of going back to "normal." The war was behind us. It was time for new things.

As president of my Jewish fraternity, I found myself working with June Alexander, the president of the Jewish sorority. A year before, when I was one of those recovering soldiers so admired by my peers, I had been invited with other soldiers to a sorority party held at June's home. It seemed like I knew everyone there except the hostess.

Now we found ourselves thrown together because of our mutual inclination toward leadership. And we discovered that the Mrs. Alexander who employed my Aunt Etta in New York was June's grandmother: another one of those small-world coincidences that pepper my life. Together we founded DU's first Hillel chapter, a coed club sponsoring social and cultural activities for Jewish students. (Hillel is still popular on many American campuses.) We even dated—but not each other. On double dates and triple dates, I would invariably find myself with June, even though she was not my date. Like any joker, I can't stand a cold silence after one of my quips. It slowly dawned on me (too slowly, according to June) that she appreciated my sense of humor more than the others. I would deliver one of my hilarious lines, and my date would barely chuckle, while June would be breaking up with laughter. I finally got smart and asked June to go out with me. It was the beginning of a romance that was to flourish.

June was a gifted and popular student, and she treasured her independence. So it was no wonder that she had no intention of letting her relatives intervene in her social life. Her grandfather, Mr. Alexander, was the sweetest old man you'd ever want to meet. He used to go regularly to the Beth HaMedrosh Hagadol (BMH) Synagogue, and he befriended a young fellow there. He would come home and tell June, "I met the nicest young man."

"Pop, don't fix me up," she'd answer, "I'll do it myself." This exchange went on week after week, as June adamantly refused to meet "the fellow" her grandfather favored.

Then one day when I picked her up for a date, I met her grandfather. A sly smile spread across his face. "June! This is the fellow I wanted you to meet!" It was true: I had been walking home from shul with him for quite awhile, and we had taken a liking to each other.

But I was in no hurry. Marriage could wait, and besides, it would break up my gang. Dave and the other guys were my social lifeline. So June and I continued to date, but I wasn't ready to take on the responsibility of a permanent relationship. I wanted to finish school and move to California.

Mother had other ideas. When June decided to attend our synagogue on Rosh Hashanah, I introduced these two women in my life to each other. After the service was over, I left June talking with my mother. When I retuned, Mother was standing alone, smiling pleasantly. I was ready to leave, but she put her hand on my arm.

"Not yet, Ivan, we have to wait for your lady friend. She went to get her coat."

"Why should we wait?"

"Well, I invited her to join us for lunch."

"You what?"

"Invited her for lunch. What's wrong with that?"

"Motherrrr!"

"What's wrong, dear?"

"You could have asked me first!"

"Whatever for? I think we'll have a lovely lunch together. Ivan, stop staring at me like that."

As it happened, she was right. It was a lovely lunch, and Mother and June laughed and talked together like old chums. I should have expected it, but I was shocked later in the year when she invited June to our Passover Seder. We weren't even engaged. I guess the guy is the last one to know.

In early December, I asked Mom to buy an engagement ring for June, and on the thirtieth of that month, I proposed. Though I hadn't planned the correlation, I realized later that was the day that I had been captured by the Germans three years before. For the second time, I was giving up my freedom on December 30.

On May 14, 1948, the last British troops left Palestine, and Israel became a state. This historical fact may seem like a digression in my personal account, but in fact, it had profound meaning for us, as it did to all Jews. It was a momentous event, uniting all the Jews in Denver, which was no small accomplishment. In fact, it probably united Jews globally, but at that point, I was focused on my own little corner of the world. June and I celebrated together, along with our friends and family, feeling a poignant joy in the victory after the recent brutal murder of six million of our people.

June and I were married on July 11, 1948.

We both graduated that spring. June received her bachelor of science degree, and I had my bachelor of fine arts. We were married a month after graduation, on July 11, 1948. I knew it then, and I still know now, that the greatest blessing I ever had was June.

When we were first married, the differences in our religious backgrounds came to the fore. June had been raised with little Jewish tradition. The Jewish world of the 1930s and '40s was much smaller than it is today, and a good Jewish education was a luxury most people simply did not have. It was not uncommon for religious and nonreligious Jews to marry and find some sort of compromise in their way of life. Although June was raised in a nonobservant home, we agreed to keep kosher and shared a deep commitment to increase our knowledge of Judaism, which would lead to further religious observances.

My new life was in full swing, and I faced the future with great optimism. At the time, the government was recruiting for the National Guard. Though many veterans flocked to join up, my response was "nothing doing!" I pushed my war experiences as far out of my mind as possible. I did not want to reminisce, as others did. I didn't want to join veterans groups or march in parades. And I swore I'd never set foot in Europe again.

CHAPTER 13

Family and Career

THERE WERE VERY FEW advertising agencies and art studios in Denver, and competition for jobs among graduating art students was fierce. My first job was assisting the resident artist and sign painter at the RKO Orpheum Theater. It paid thirty-two dollars per week, enough to live on since we were rent free.

This was a time before television, so the local movie theater was a major form of family entertainment. Every large theater had its own studio that produced signs for the front of the theater, advertising the weekly new movie. Depending on the importance of the coming film, we created some very elaborate and spectacular fronts, huge banners, lobby displays, and newspapers ads. I was working in a field quite removed from my commercial art training, but it was a fascinating departure.

I signed up for evening classes in a technical school, with my tuition covered by the GI Bill. I took courses in sign painting and silk-screen printing, a commercial printing process used for producing signs, banners, and decals in quantity. I could see great possibilities in the techniques I was learning in school.

After six months, I went to the manager of the Orpheum and asked for a raise. My salary went up to thirty-seven dollars per week, but June and I soon realized that would never be enough. Our first baby was on the way, and we had to find our own apartment. I decided to quit my job and take a calculated risk: I opened my own sign and silk-screen business, Display Art Sign Company.

My in-laws allowed me to use part of their large basement as my first studio. At first with a partner, then on my own, I created signs, banners, and posters. June and I were able to move into our own apartment, paying fifty dollars a month. This was a great deal of money to us, but we needed our own place—somewhere we could build our family and establish our own lifestyle. In October 1949, our first child, Michael Jay, was born. Like all new parents, we thought of him as a tiny miracle.

The income from my business gradually increased, and I rented a small building. Our second son, David Alan, was born three years later. My business was moved to larger quarters, and our family went to a two-bedroom apartment.

How the wheel of fortune can turn! In time, the Orpheum Theater closed its art and sign department, and I took my former boss as a partner. Eventually, I bought out his share, and he became my employee. Silk-screen printing became more and more popular, and some theater artists started a company called Denver Advertising. I merged my company with theirs under the name Advertising Display Company.

There were other commercial silk-screen businesses operating in Denver, and the question was how to beat the competition. I bought state-of-the-art machinery, printing presses that would reduce the need for hand lettering. We were the first in Denver to use this kind of machine. I still kept one department for hand lettering, but the printing press became the mainstay of the business and was a huge success. We did convention displays and exhibits, and advertising agencies gave us assignments. I enjoyed the work immensely. It is a great blessing when one can do work that is truly satisfying.

Our third son, Daniel Seth, was born two years after David, and our fourth and last child, Judith Sue, was born two and a half years later. My business moved for the third time to larger quarters and our own building. I strongly felt that I should pass on to my children the invaluable knowledge, experience, and responsibility I had learned working with my mother at Murph's. As they grew up, all of our children worked at the Advertising Display Company. Just as I had learned many essential lessons in my youth, they too learned much that they could apply to their future lives.

The fact that I had been a soldier continued to give us benefits that made life easier. June and I purchased our first home with a GI loan, and we moved to a larger house with plenty of room for the children to play. I was fully aware that all of my good fortune had been provided by the same Partner who had protected Mother. Though I allowed my nightmarish memories to recede in my mind, I never forgot the vow I had made in that packed cattle car in Germany.

We became close to a young rabbi who arrived in Denver around the time that June and I were just starting out. We joined his fledgling traditional congregation, for it seemed to me that now that I was settled, with my own family and business, I could dedicate more time to learning about Judaism. Rabbi Daniel and Ida Goldberger were the same age as June and I; they proved to be great lifelong friends and true catalysts for our spiritual growth. From the beginning, Mother also took a great liking to them and invited them to her home. They were honored guests at our family Thanksgiving meal, and from then on, it became a tradition for them to join our family for this event every year.

Fresh from rabbinical school in Skokie, Illinois, Rabbi Goldberger came from a long line of rabbis and knew what it meant to build a congregation. It is certainly not only a matter of leading prayers or giving sermons. A rabbi is a mentor, a confidant, and an advocate. It's not an easy life, especially if a rabbi is conscientious about being there for everybody, at all hours, seven days a week—and Rabbi Goldberger was as dedicated as any rabbi could be. Starting out in a small rented hall on the East Side of Denver with Torahs from a synagogue that had closed, he attracted more and more congregants. He was a master at taking families that had little or no connection to Judaism and leading them toward deeper appreciation of their heritage.

His manner was direct but not aggressive. He was a wonderful teacher who brought meaning into everything. He was inspiring and magnetic, and his approach was reasonable. Knowing that becoming an observant Jew means taking on a great many lifestyle changes, he never pushed anyone to commit to total observance. He knew that once a person starts to keep one commandment, does one mitzvah, he or she would move on to the others.

Denver had an outstanding Jewish education program in which rabbis and teachers across the spectrum of Jewish life taught various classes. Rabbi Goldberger's classes were always filled. We know. We went to all of them.

His congregation grew quite large, and after much fundraising, a building was constructed. My shul finally had its own home. But the rabbi wouldn't let us rest on the satisfaction of building a structure. He stressed that along with communal growth, we must each keep growing within ourselves too. He formed a study group of six couples who met once a month. We read and discussed Jewish books on philosophy, faith, and Jewish living. Sometime we agreed, sometimes we debated, and often we found ourselves needing more research to answer the questions that arose. It was an enriching, growing experience. It was a way of exploring every facet of Judaism using our intellects, our experiences, and our gut feelings. June and I appreciated every aspect of the meetings, and we enjoyed the social camaraderie. With increased Jewish knowledge, came increased commitment. Little by little, we found ourselves becoming more Orthodox in our outlook and more observant of Jewish laws.

Our children now attended a Jewish day school, and we needed to keep up with them. June and I went to more classes on Judaism, steadily becoming more and more observant and finding great satisfaction in the lifestyle. Ultimately, we would move to a strictly Orthodox shul, though our deep friendship with the Goldbergers never abated.

Mother, of course, was delighted with this development, and she heartily endorsed our decision to send the children to a school where they would receive an intensive Jewish education. She always made it a point to attend the school's fundraising dinners, and she did so proudly.

In fact, she always gave charity with a full heart, thankful that her lifelong Partner had never failed her. The woman who collected donations for Israel on behalf of the

As adults, my brothers and I cherished Mother even more than when we were children, for we understood and respected her unerring values and priorities. She never ceased to inspire us with her example. Standing, left to right: Jerome, Max, and me.

Allied Jewish Federation of Colorado always knew that
Mrs. Goldstein would be waiting for her, money in hand.
There was no need for pledges; she just gave, and with such
gratitude on her face that the collector said, "She always
made me feel like I was doing her a favor!"

So it came as a shock to the entire Denver Jewish
community when Mother passed away. The year was
1972. June and I, together with two other couples,
Sally and Dave Spivak and Helen and Al Markson, had
been planning our first trip to Israel. For me, it would
be more than a vacation; I had looked forward to this
visit as an emotional and spiritual opportunity for
many years. As a young boy, I had listened enraptured
as Mother read stories from the Bible, learning about
the covenant that God made with our people and our
inseparable connection with the land of Israel. With the
establishment of the state of Israel in 1948, my dream
of visiting grew stronger and stronger. Now it was going
to become a reality.

But we delayed our trip because Mother seemed to
be having problems with internal bleeding. Despite our
urging her to see a doctor, she insisted that she felt fine
and refused to go. After more pleading and pressure, she
went to a doctor, who predictably wanted her admitted to
the hospital for tests. She refused, citing the fact that she
hadn't been a patient in a hospital in forty-two years, since
Max was born. Perhaps remembering my father's untimely
death after a routine dental procedure, she made it plain

that she didn't trust doctors and feared that she would never leave the hospital alive.

But there was no alternative. Ultimately, she had to go to for tests, and an intestinal tumor was found. It was removed, and the results were promising. She was to return home in a few days. But a blockage occurred, her complaints were ignored, and gangrene set in. To the end, she was a fighter and never gave up hope. But it proved to be too much for her.

News of the death of Ida Goldstein was in the Denver newspapers and set off an enormous emotional reaction throughout the city. Privately, our family knew well what an unusually resolute and positive person she had been. Despite all of the truly bitter events of her life, she never turned cynical or despairing. She faced those challenges as they came to her, like waves hitting a rocky shore, and stood up to them with a faith and determination. Her goal of raising her children and instilling in them the values that she treasured had been accomplished.

As my brothers and I married and eventually provided her with ten grandchildren, she joyfully emerged as the greatest bubbie. She told her grandchildren stories, read to them, encouraged them to develop their talents, and gave out treats (especially Life Savers and lemon drops). As they grew older, they discovered what a wise and wonderful confidant she could be.

Years ago, my friends and my brothers' friends had discovered this quality in our Mom, and they often stopped

Friends Mourn Passing of Mrs. Goldstein

Mrs. Ida Goldstein

An anchor of inner security to her family, Ida Goldstein was a true Jewish woman of valor —revered by her children and her grandchildren.

She was a women who achieved real nachas through her children.

Rabbi Jerome Lipsitz of Beth Joseph, speaking at funeral services held Feb. 25 at Feldman Chapel told the large crowd of mourners "Ida met grief in life with courage and fortitude. She passed her love for Judaism and for Israel on to her sons, all of whom have become leaders.

"Jerry is a leading philanthropist for the State of Israel and Jewish organizations; Ivan is a past president of Hillel Academy

and of the Beth Joseph Ritual committee and Mordecai (Max) is a leading cantor in Haddonofield, N.J."

In speaking to the friends who had gathered, Rabbi Manuel Laderman said "In Israel two phrases are used—to make immortal and to join together. Ida Goldstein had a special committment of unity and the impressive numbers here today indicate their unity with the family, by loving and caring in remembering."

A personal friend of the Goldsteins since coming to Denver 20 years ago, Rabbi Daniel Goldberger added a tender, personal note when he recalled that the first Thanksgiving he and his family spent in Denver was at the Goldstein home and each year since that time they had always spent the holiday together.

"Her death parallels her life —a struggle in courage," said Rabbi Goldberger, adding this was her first time in a hospital since the birth of her youngest son.

A member of a pioneer Denver family, her grandfather came to Denver in the early 1880's in a covered wagon. Married in 1920, she was widowed in 1930. She and her late husband owned "Murph's" Jewelers for 52 years.

"Each Shabbos for the next four weeks reveals that no one is complete within themselves," added Rabbi Goldberger. The first Shabbos tells of sharing with others and is the Shabbos of remembrance. She remembered hatred and injustice to others and always spoke against this. The second Shabbos is of righteousness, which she expressed through her open indignation against prejudice.

Third is the Shabbos declaring faith in G-d. Mrs. Goldstein was a true lover of Judaism, an avid reader she was always eager to learn more. Fourth, the Shabbos prior to Passover is one of springtime and new hope. She epitomized hope and optimism and continuously renewed herself.

In addition to her three children, she is survived by eleven grandchildren.

Burial was in Rose Hill Cemetery.

Contributions may be made to Hillel Academy.

by Murph's for a private chat with her. She would guide them through their recent heartaches, advise them on employment, and inspire them to seek solutions to their problems. Years later, as her grandchildren grew, they too would stop at the store to have long discussions with their Bubbie. They brought their friends, and soon a new generation of young people sought her counsel. She would listen patiently, and they knew beyond doubt that she would always be discreet, never revealing their confidences to anyone. This kind of trust is rare in teenagers, but Bubbie Goldstein was an exception to every rule.

Mother was eulogized by five rabbis, including our beloved Rabbi Goldberger. Though she had little money and had been unassuming all her life, she was given the honors of a notable. Our family had no idea of the extent of her reach and how many people she had helped in her lifetime. Now those people were coming forward   huge numbers of men and women who came to the shiva, telling story after story that amazed even us. As word of her demise rippled outward, letters started arriving. At least fifty people whose names were totally unfamiliar to us wrote to tell us of the extraordinary things she had done for them, what a caring person she was, that she was one of the kindest and most unusual people they had ever met.

And Mother had saved a few surprises for me too. All of her life, she worked so hard at the store that I wanted to help her out financially once I was able. Though she continued to work, I gave her a check every week so she would know that she could retire whenever the time was right. It wasn't until she died that I realized that she had never cashed any of my checks.

One of her most poignant posthumous gifts hearkened back to my childhood. When I was a youngster, my parents spoke Yiddish—the traditional tongue of Eastern European Jews—so my brothers and I would learn the language of our heritage. Mother would take us to see Yiddish movies, seat us in the back of the theater (so we wouldn't disturb anyone), and then translate the dialogue. In Yiddish, there is an expression for everything, words of wisdom as well as silly sayings, and Mother used them all. "A fool is half a prophet," she would murmur mysteriously, leaving us to figure out what that meant. Although I never learned to speak Yiddish, I memorized many of the colorful expressions, folk songs, and words or wisdom.

Toward the end of her life, I asked her to write down all of these expressions so I could learn them. She said she would try. I forgot about it. But Mother always kept a promise. After her death, we found a little notebook in her handwriting titled "For Ivan." It was a list of transliterated Yiddish expressions, with full translations.

Two months after Mother's death, we took our planned trip to Israel. My friend Dave and I visited my grandfather's grave, a moving experience for us both. As I anticipated, treading on the holy soil of Israel made me feel even more rooted to my ancestors and their religious lifestyle. We promised ourselves we would come back to explore Israel again, and we returned to Denver inspired to further study our heritage.

Moving steadily into a more religious lifestyle did not mean that we would abandon our cherished friends, however. My army buddy Andy Urda and I kept our friendship intact, as we had always known we would. As prisoners, we had fixated on what life would be like after the war. He said he had a job waiting for him when he got back to the Ford Motor Company steel plant in Michigan—and he did. Over the years, Andy and his family visited us in Denver, we took trips together, and our wives and children became close friends.

On the Urdas' first trip to Denver, we had a barbecue at our house, and my mother and brothers were invited to meet Andy and his family. Andy's wish to meet Mother finally materialized. He spent the entire evening talking to Mother, and it was like he had been reunited with a person he had always known.

Though we were in contact every few months, we didn't talk about the war. I wanted to forget it, and Andy had never quite got over the trauma we endured. He never slept a peaceful night and was in psychiatric treatment for the rest of his life. I was not aware of the depth of his agony until his children revealed it to me, but I did know that we were still bonded together at many levels. One night in 1979, June and I were going to the theater, and I told her that I had a strong urge to call Andy. But we were in a hurry, and she suggested that I call him tomorrow. The next day, before I could call, the phone rang. It was Andy's daughter, Alene.

"Ivan, I don't know how to tell you this . . ."

"It's about your father! Something happened to Andy, didn't it?"

"Why, yes. How did you know?"

"What happened? Can I speak to him?"

"Ivan, my dad had open-heart surgery yesterday and . . . and he died on the table."

"I wish I had known he was having the surgery."

"That's my fault, Ivan—I'm so sorry! The night before, he said to me, 'I've got to call Ivan,' and I told him 'Call tomorrow, when the surgery is over.' It's my fault he didn't call—Dad really wanted you to know!"

"In a way, I did know. Don't worry yourself about it. He was a good man and a true friend. He was a brave man too. You know, he never let the Germans know how much he was suffering, always stood up as straight as he could, always tried to look like he was fine. He felt that he represented all Americans, and he had to prove that we're not weaklings or complainers. He carried himself like a hero, Alene."

"I know. I think you understood him better than anybody."

"I'll miss him terribly. Thank you for making this difficult phone call. Please give my condolences to Helen, Andrea, and Greg."

That night, during dinner, our family talked about Andy and his family. The conversation evoked suppressed and forgotten memories of our shared captivity. When the family went to bed, I sat in the dark living room for hours, thinking about Andy, and our desperate survival, our conversations, our joy at liberation, our bond. In four months, we had become one, and now a part of me had died. I felt that the last vestige of my war experience was now gone.

But that was not quite true. In March 1983, June and I were preparing to go to Israel to spend Passover with our son David, by now a Jerusalem resident with his own family. There were so many details I had to take care of at work, and I was in the middle a very hectic day. My secretary buzzed me and said that I had a call waiting on line two. The caller wouldn't identify himself, but insisted that it was very important. I picked up the phone, and an unfamiliar voice asked, "Is this Ivan Goldstein?"

"Yes. Who is this?"

"A voice from your past. Where were you thirty-eight years ago this coming Wednesday?"

"I am not that fast at math, and I have no idea; you tell me."

"Nineteen forty-five."

"I was still in the army."

"Correct. And do you know what annual event will take place eight days from tonight?"

I thought to myself, who is this joker? I don't have time to play games. But I tried to keep from being rude. The voice said, "Think. What's on your calendar?"

"It will be the first night of Passover."

"Correct. Now where were you on the first day of Passover, 1945?"

"You tell me!" I exploded.

"You were in Stalag XII A, in Limburg, Germany. That's when you were liberated, though you didn't know what day it was."

"How do you know?"

"Because I was with you."

A cold chill went through me.

"The name is Schwartz," he said at length, "Murray Schwartz. I was with you in the prison camp and also the hospitals after liberation."

"I . . . I'm sorry. I remember very little about what happened. I don't even remember your name."

"Oh, I know," he answered gently, "you were very sick, but you talked a lot in the hospital."

Could it be? Was this the other American who shared the sick room with Andy and me?

"You're the guy who yelled 'The Americans are here!'"

"Yes."

June and I met with Murray and his wife in New York before our flight to Tel Aviv. During the long dinner, he filled in details and events of my last days at Stalag XII A and the early days at the hospital: things I could never recollect on my own. The more he spoke about his war experiences, the more apparent it was that they had become a critical part of his present life. Instead of leaving memories behind him, as I had, he seemed almost obsessed with reliving them. He told me that he had been back to Germany four times and had retraced his steps as a prisoner. His research on the subject was endless, and he collected photos and memorabilia of the era. I discovered that people react to bad experiences in many different ways.

It was fascinating to learn, however, that the date of our liberation was Thursday, March 29, 1945, on the Hebrew calendar the fifteenth of Nisan, the first day of Passover. Every year at the Seder, Jews recount the numerous instances of release from bondage that miraculously occurred on that date throughout our long history. Ever since my talk with Murray, in my mind I have gratefully added the liberation of Stalag XII A to the list.

But other than that annual thanksgiving, I felt that the fewer reminders there were, the better. The horrors of my war experiences were hard to forget but even harder to remember. After speaking with Murray, I felt sure that the war was now out of my life for good. There was no way I could have expected another astonishing relic to reappear, but it did—for out of the mists of time emerged none other than my old tank, the *Barracuda*.

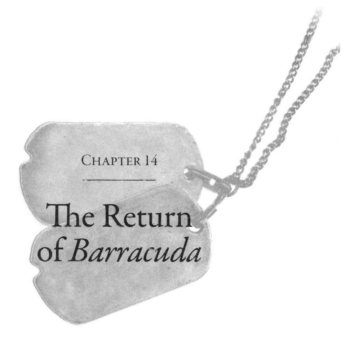

CHAPTER 14

The Return of *Barracuda*

THE UNCANNY STORY BEGINS in 1947, when the landscape of Europe was covered with destroyed army vehicles. Villagers and scrap dealers came with acetylene torches and cut up whatever they could find to be sold as scrap metal. An American M4 Sherman tank sat rusting in a meadow pond in Millomont, Belgium. Mr. Denis, the owner of the meadow, was afraid that cutting up the tank would contaminate the ecology of his natural spring. The government removed the severely damaged tank intact and gave it to the people of Bastogne, recognizing that the nearby town had become a famous symbol of resistance in the Battle of the Bulge.

Mounted on a pedestal in McAuliffe Square, it was a monument to the bravery of the American forces that

The *Barracuda*, now serving as a memorial to the Battle of the Bulge, 1944–1945, stands in Bastogne's McAuliffe Square.

liberated the town from the German grip in that deadly winter of 1945. It was revered as a memorial to the victory of good over evil, a symbol of freedom.

For nearly fifty years, tourists from around the world came with their cameras and took triumphant pictures in front of this monument without knowing any details of its role in the Bulge. They looked at the gaping hole slashed by Nazi shells through the thick armor plating on its left flank and at another puncture at the rear of the tank, and they wondered if the men in this tank had survived. Identifying markings had been erased by time and weather. To which Army unit did the tank belong? Who were the men who had manned it during its last desperate moments in battle?

A good many rumors circulated from time to time. Some said that the 4th Armored Division broke through the German defense of Bastogne, and this was the first tank, Lieutenant Boggess' tank. Others said it was undoubtedly the tank that General George Patton himself rode in when he entered Bastogne. Dramatic tales such as these, true or not, sheathed the tank in glory.

In 1996, the Cercle d'Histoire de Bastogne (Bastogne Historical Society) decided to solve this mystery. A historian from the organization, Roger Marquet, placed a letter in the *Bulge Bugle*, the official newsletter of veterans of the Battle of the Bulge. He was seeking information regarding the crew of this now-famous tank. His chances of finding the crew were pretty slim, though his research had already revealed some information. In his letter, he spelled out his theory that, judging from its location, the tank had to belong to the 11th Armored Division. According to a witness, it had been hit and taken out of action at Millomont Pond on December 30, 1944. The crew all got out of the fiery tank, but it was unknown what happened to them after that. Did anyone from this crew survive, and if so, were any of them alive in 1996, fifty-two years later?

I was seventy-two years old by then. June and I had moved to Jerusalem permanently, and I had no interest in reading the *Bugle*. But during a visit to Denver in the summer of 1997—a year after Marquet wrote his letter—my cousin Howard Greinetz asked me if I remembered the date that I was captured by the Germans.

11TH ARMORED DIVISION VERSUS FUHRER BEGLEIT BRIGADE

Well known tank looking for its courageous crew

If tourists enjoy taking pictures of a Sherman tank, it is without any doubt the one located on McAuliffe Square at Bastogne, Belgium. The tank's number and its seven victory bars seem to be genuine. This tank wears the 4th Armored Division colors and signs. This glorious division made a break into Bastogne encirclement on December 26, 1944. But, in fact, this Sherman was part of the 11th Armored Division. Here is its story...

After the war ended, some scrap merchants began to cut out the tank wrecks which lay strewn about the Bastogne area battlefields. Everyone of them, except one! The one located in Mr. Denis' meadow at Hubermont. The meadow's owner was firmly opposed to cutting it with the blowlamp on site, because he was afraid of a probable pollution of a close spring. So, this wrecked vehicle remained there for several months until someone decided to bring it to McAuliffe Square at Bastogne, as a commemorating monument of the Battle of the Bulge.

Mr. Reisen's Story

A direct witness of what happened to that Sherman, Mr. Reisen, who is still living in the Village of Hubermont, told us:

"One day around 3:00 p.m., a U.S. tank coming from Rechrival direction, appeared at the Hubermont crossroads; it went down the road's banking and into a field and drove towards Renuamont. We suddenly heard a big noise. (It could have been an explosion.) After that, the tank came back by the same way. When it arrived close to the brook, its wheels began to spin and it got stuck in the mud.

"A German tank had located it and was following it. This German tank stopped right in front of my home, shot one shell and the American tank was hit in its left flank. The German crew got out of their tank and ran towards the Sherman which was 200 yards away.

"An E.M. probably badly injured, was immediately finished off by the Germans. A second one was carried out in a blanket into the closest bushes and also finished off with a hand gun. The third one, who seemed to be fine, was taken as a prisoner. The last two crew members, who tried to hide themselves in the water of a pond, were taken off towards Hubermont crossroads, along with the first prisoner."

Mr. Reisen does not remember anymore what day it occurred but he is sure of one thing: it happened before January 1, 1945, because on that day his home burned to the ground.

We know that the 42nd Tank Battalion of the 11th Armored Division attacked that area on January 1, but we do not know who was the Sherman's crew. That event probably occurred on December 30, 1944.

Otto Reimer's Testimony— Fuhrer Begleit Brigade's Commander— December 30, 1944

...As I noticed an enemy task force progressing north through Lavaselle towards Rechrival, that meant in the direction of our poor defensive security line, I immediately ran into my personal command car, and I drove through the "Bois des Valets" towards Renuamont where my staff brigade moved in that morning. As I was talking with my chief of staff about the engagement, the first enemy tank had already driven by the staff building and the second one was close to the Hubermont church. This first tank was destroyed by an antitank grenade and the second one was obliged to withdraw. An assault guns company--still available--was sent from Millomont to southwest to make a blockroad on the south of Rechrival and to hold the area on between that road and "Bois des Valets."

Suppositions

These two witnesses are undoubtedly describing the same scene, but seen from both sides. The tank on the hill of Renuamont (close to the Fuhrer Begleit Brigade Staff) was hit the first time by a Panzerfaust. With or without engine, it managed to drive down the hill where it got stuck in the mud. At that moment, it was hit a second time by a German "Hetzer" nestling against Mr Reisen's front house.

Questions

1. It seems that there were two men killed and three survivors. These three survivors were probably taken as POW's. Who were they? Are they still alive today? (We would be pleased if some one would advise us about them.)
2. What were the original signs on that tank? Maybe it belonged to the 41st Tank Battalion, 11th Armored Division? Not sure! But, if it is, the two victims could be Hansen and Spero from Company D. Who were the three others? It could also belong to the 42nd Tank Battalion. We can still discern a round shield above the left track. With a magnifying glass, it seems to be the letters T and H...for Thunderbolts?
3. That tank has seven victory bars in its White Star. We know the 11th Armored jumped off on December 30. Do we have to conclude that the tank got seven victories in one day?
4. The serial number on the tank is still the same as in 1944: 3081532.

Anybody who has information about this event is asked to write to: Roger Marquet - Fonds de Foret 67, 4870 Trooz, Belgium.

Submitted by:
Jacques DeGrive & Roger Marquet
CRIBA - Belgium

[Our members would also be interested in following up on this matter. So, if you write to Roger with any details, make a copy for us. Thanks.]

The letter Roger Marquet placed in the *Bulge Bugle* seeking to find the crew of the unknown tank.

"December 30, 1944. Why do you ask?"

"Look at this, Ivan," he said, leaning forward with a copy of the *Bulge Bugle.* I read Marquet's letter half-heartedly.

"So?"

"So it sounds like your tank!"

"Howard, there were thousands of Shermans in Europe. What are the chances?"

"Ivan, it's become an international landmark! Don't you want to call the historian?"

"Not especially. Who wants to relive all that?"

But I took the paper with me and said I would call the phone number when I returned to Jerusalem. I took it home and promptly forgot about it.

A couple of months later, June reminded me about the ad and insisted that I call. I phoned that evening and listened to a recorded voice in French. I didn't understand it, but I figured I'd leave my message anyway: "My name is Ivan Goldstein. I live in Jerusalem, Israel. I read your letter in the *Bulge Bugle.* I believe I am a member of the crew that you are looking for."

Later that evening, the phone rang, and the excited caller said in English, "I am Roger Marquet." He asked questions, and I answered for about forty minutes. From my responses, he said that it sounded like the tank in Bastogne indeed was the *Barracuda.* He said that I would hear from him again shortly.

Within a week, Roger called and asked me if I would come to Bastogne for a special ceremony and dedication of the tank. My answer was a firm no. I had no intention of returning to Belgium, Germany, or any part of Europe. He asked me to reconsider my decision, adding that it would be a very thrilling and prestigious celebration. What's more, he said, he believed that I was the only living survivor of the crew.

I stood fast. But a groundswell of pressure arose from my family. My children and grandchildren, my cousins, even my friends, all told me that it would be the experience of a lifetime. Of that, I was sure, and I wasn't at all anxious to have it.

My twelve-year-old grandson made the breakthrough. David's fourth child, Natan, frequently came to our home. He was sincerely interested in hearing about the war and was fascinated by the discovery of my tank. He kept telling me, "Zaidy, you and Bubbie should really plan to go back for the celebration. You really should." And he wouldn't give up. He kept asking me, respectfully, but with his strong Goldstein persistence.

Natan's Bar Mitzvah was coming up. I gave in and told him that for his Bar Mitzvah present we would take him to Belgium for the event, but, unfortunately, he would have to miss a week of school. He was elated, and missing school was an added bonus. I called Roger and told him our decision, requesting that they not plan the program until after our Passover in April. Well advertised on television, radio, and in newspapers, the program was planned as a three-day gala celebration, beginning on May 8, 1998, the week of V-E Day celebrations.

On the morning of May 8, Natan, June, and I arrived by train in Bastogne from Brussels. The lush green countryside was a shocking contrast to my first arrival there fifty-four years earlier. The enduring image in my mind was one of ice and snow, bare trees bending to blasts of arctic winds. Nazi gunfire was our blistering welcome.

But now it was a beautiful, sunny day. We were greeted warmly and taken to our hotel, bordering McAuliffe Square. The three of us walked to the tank. I have to admit that I approached it with some trepidation, almost hoping that this wasn't the *Barracuda*. But I knew the instant I saw it. For the first time, I saw the two gaping holes made by the shells that had finished off my tank. I pictured myself deep in fierce concentration, firing the bow gun for hours as Andy maneuvered us round and round enemy tanks. I could envision us battling through village after village. And I remembered the last time I saw the *Barracuda,* a fiery mass, as I was being led away into captivity.

Now the tank sat motionless on her platform in the public square, seemingly frozen in time. She had been repainted, and her guns pointed abstractly into the past. The smoke of battle, the cries of the wounded; the entire bloody scenario etched into my memory was long gone. There were only children playing and tourists sipping Cokes as they looked up at it in admiration. People walked around us, glancing benignly at me, likely wondering why the eyes of the elderly gent were moist.

As I showed the tank to June and Natan, it was hard to believe that it was really the *Barracuda*.

Three historians, Roger Marquet, Jacques Degive, and Robert Fergloute, met us at the tank and took us to the Maison Mathelin War Museum. After the visit, I retold the story of December 30 and how the tank was knocked out of commission by enemy fire, and details of my interrogation in the German headquarters near the tank. After reviewing my testimony, the three historians tried to establish, without doubt, that the tank on the square was the *Barracuda*, for when the tank was repainted, the name was covered. Jacques Degive was more skeptical than the other two; he seemed rather unconvinced that the tank in the square was mine. In telling my story, I mentioned the wooden box behind my seat that contained candy bars and chewing gum. In the next few days, this bit of information would become quite valuable.

We were then taken to other World War II sites and monuments. A special luncheon followed, with many journalists, photographers, media people, and city officials. The next day, there was a brief ceremony at the tank. We then moved on to the town hall, where the mayor and his officials presented me with a medal and a gift. We were told to prepare ourselves for the parade the next day, May 10. I wasn't sure how to prepare myself, for I had no idea what was coming.

I soon found out. The town of Bastogne had prepared a hero's welcome beyond my wildest dreams. There was a large procession of restored American army vehicles—jeeps, command cars, and trucks—with the drivers outfitted in World War II American uniforms. June, Natan, and I were in the lead jeep. (I've never seen my grandson's face glow as it did that day.) The convoy retraced the *Barracuda*'s journey of December 30 over the hills and valleys and through the towns and villages where we had fought. Townspeople, schoolchildren, choirs, and bands gathered to meet our convoy as we rolled through. Businesses closed, and people lined the streets, waving flags and cheering. You would think that I had personally liberated Belgium!

The Belgian Medal of Valor (front and back).

The procession started at Jodenville and ended at Renuamont, passing through Morhet, Poisson-Moulin, Lavaselle, Brul, Houmont, and Sainte-Ode, where a special ceremony and program took place. It included most of the citizens, schoolchildren, and a band. In each town, the mayor and town officials greeted us. There were speeches, flowers, and fanfare wherever we went. It took the entire day.

The most emotionally jarring stop was in Rechimont, at Mr. Oger Lhoas's farm. This was where the German head-quarters was located and I spent my first miserable night as a prisoner, expecting to be executed in the morning. Mr. Lhoas and many residents, including Edouard Reisen,

The Belgian Fiftieth Anniversary Medal for the Battle of the Bulge (front and back). The original ribbons were lost.

were waiting for us. Mr. Reisen was the only civilian witness to the destruction of the *Barracuda*. He knew for a fact that December 30 was the date of its destruction, as much of his family's farm was demolished by shells on that day. A teenager at the time, he crouched behind his barn watching the battle and saw the *Barracuda* mired in the pond in the valley below. He saw two soldiers jump out of the burning tank (Urda and me). It was amazing to me that I met with Mr. Reisen at all. He had lived on the farm his entire life. Now seventy, he had recently sold it and was to move away that night. What a providential coincidence of timing, I thought. I had arrived just in time to meet and talk with him on his final day there.

As soon as the people heard him tell his version of my story, they crowded around, bombarding me with questions and more questions. Through an interpreter, I answered as many as I could. Then came the question that was to establish, once and for all, the identity of the tank as truly mine. The grandson of the farm's owner said that as a boy, he used to play in the tank—and he asked me why there were so many gum and candy wrappers pasted inside its walls! I told him that I had stored a lot of candy, and when the tank was on fire the shells inside probably exploded, throwing the candy in all directions with such impact that the wrappers stayed stuck to the walls. That was enough proof for Monsieur Degive. (Later, serial numbers were checked and verified.) The historian was quite sure that no one could make up that detail. He beamed with delight.

I had decided to stop fighting the memories, at least for today. I asked if I could see the barn where we were held as prisoners. They took me to a barn, and I looked around in puzzlement. This was not the place. I remembered it as very small and cramped. That night before my intended execution, I had studied every board of it, every knothole in the floor. I was then told that the barn had been enlarged, but it still didn't fit in with my memories. Something was wrong and troubling; this was not the tiny hut I remembered. In fact, the answer to my dilemma would not emerge until two years later.

The farmhouse, converted to German headquarters,
where we were interrogated.

We went to the farmhouse on the ridge where I had
stood as a prisoner facing the German commander. I clearly
recalled that you had to go up three or four steps to enter
the building, and, in fact, they were right there. Why did I
remember the steps? I must have been acutely aware of them
at the time because my leg wound was in pain. Yet, everything else about it seemed so changed that I again said it
wasn't the same place. The historians looked dubiously from
one to the other, until the owner recalled that they since had
added on to the building and changed the windows.

203

After leaving the farm, we walked to the pasture between Hubermont and Renuamont, to the spot where the *Barracuda* had been stopped. The Millomont Pond was now just a swampy green area, nearly dry, with wild grass growing everywhere. And there was no snow, no gunfire, no freezing wind. As I stood there, I closed my eyes, and the hazy screen blocking my memories lifted, revealing a time long gone. Fifty-four years slipped away in an instant; I had to fight back the tears. I saw myself—just a kid—springing out of the tank and running along the top, smelling the acrid fumes of gunpowder and burning oil, hearing the ping of bullets ricocheting off the tank beneath me. I shivered for a second, once again feeling the plunge into the dark, icy water and the pounding of my heart as I hoped, prayed, that the Germans would not find me.

Then I opened my eyes and gazed up at the farmhouse where Andy and I had carried Wally Alexander. I did not have to recall. The experience was as alive to me as if it had just happened. My eyes and Mr. Reisen's met for a few seconds, and it was plain to me that we were both reliving that moment.

We plodded up the other side of the valley to his house, where we were able to visualize the German guns firing the crippling hit on the *Barracuda*. They certainly had an easy shot at us.

In our last official event we were taken to the Peace Forest for a tree planting ceremony. A small plaque was installed at the base of each tree bearing the name of some

A tree-planting ceremony, with me at the left and
Roger Marquet at the right.

GI who had participated in the liberation of Belgium.
The "Star Spangled Banner" played in the background
as my plaque was unveiled. To my surprise it did not say
"Denver" or "U.S.A." beneath my name and division, but
"Israel." I was very proud and happy.

Traveling back to Houmont, the historians were in a
festive mood. Their fifty-year-old mystery of the McAuliffe
Square tank had been solved. But for me, memories I had
long suppressed had risen sharply to the surface. At first,
I felt saddened, sorry that all the pain I had so successfully buried throughout my life had been conjured. But
on reflection, I felt that it had been good to evoke these

The plaque at the base of my tree.

memories once again, for only then could I truly appreciate and readdress my thankfulness to God for the many times during my captivity that He delivered me from harm. This occasion, indeed, was a time to remember.

Every morning, in our prayers, Jews recite the Thirtieth Psalm. Written by King David, who was no stranger to mortal danger, the last part of the psalm reads, "To You, God, I would call. . . . What gain is there in my death, when I descend to the pit? . . . Hear [me] God, and favor me. Lord, be my helper! You have changed my lament into dancing. . . . You undid my sackcloth and girded me with gladness. So that my soul might sing to You and not be stilled, my God, forever will I thank You!" I couldn't have said it better myself.

Over the three-day celebration, we became especially good friends with Roger, the historian who had brought us there. The gracious and overwhelming reception we received was hard to believe. As we were leaving Bastogne, our hosts asked Natan what the most impressive thing that he experienced during the three days was. His immediate response surprised me: "The respect and admiration the people showed my grandfather." And he looked at me with a new light in his eyes. It was worth the trip.

CHAPTER 15

Belgium Revisited

ODDLY ENOUGH, seeing the *Barracuda* again and reliving the emotions of that fateful day in 1944 fortified me in ways I could never have predicted. From the safe distance of a fifty-year separation, I was ready to cope with the memories, deal with the pain, and move on. In fact, I became curious about my old army buddies.

Roger Marquet turned out to be an excellent resource. He had spoken to the families of several of the men I had known, and he surprised me with his revelations. Dage Hebert, whom I couldn't find at all after I jumped from the tank, suffered leg wounds, was sent to a German army hospital, and had survived. But Ed Mattson—the lone survivor of the other tank, who had a serious wound in his hand—died as a prisoner of war. Most shocking of all was that Cecil Peterman was alive! On the day I was captured, I had seen him lying face down in the snow and watched in horror as they turned over his body and yanked the hunting knife off his belt. It turned out that he had not been dead, just badly wounded and unconscious. I didn't see the Germans take him to their hospital. Like me, he wound up in Stalag XII A, and he lived to tell the tale.

When I heard Peterman was alive, I called him on the phone, anxious to see him again. But he lived in Oklahoma, and he wasn't well enough to travel. He told me that after the war, he had gone back to Bastogne and seen the tank in McAuliffe Square, but he had no idea it was the *Barracuda*. He told me that he and Wally Alexander had been taken to the same German army hospital. He knew, as I did, that Wally had died of his terrible wounds.

I wondered about the others. Whatever happened to Ed Kessler, who had bravely spoken up for me when the German commander ordered, "Kill the Jew"? And Ed Lozano, who stuck with Kessler as his partner and had slipped out of Gerolstein on my train ticket? I knew that Lozano had survived, because he visited me at Fitzsimons hospital, but I had lost track of him. Were they still alive now?

My trip to Belgium and the ensuing publicity about my tank proved to be the key to answering these questions. In 1998, the summer after my visit to Bastogne, June and I returned to Denver for our annual family visit. My children there told me that Tom Williams, a World War II historian from Wisconsin, had heard the story of the *Barracuda* and wanted to talk to me. I called him. We spoke for a while, and he later came to Denver to interview me.

Tom's particular expertise was in the 101st Airborne Division, known as the "Screaming Eagles," the subject of many books and a movie. When I heard this, I asked him if he could find my fellow captives from the 101st— Lozano and Kessler. The next day, he called me back and told me that not only were they alive, but that he had their addresses and phone numbers.

When I connected with Ed Kessler, he nearly fainted. He had been firmly convinced that Urda and I both perished in Stalag XII A before the liberation. When I told him, "This is your old friend, Ivan Goldstein," he could barely answer. After he got over the initial shock, we had several long, satisfying talks. I learned that he had lied about his age in order to enlist. He was only seventeen at the time, and he had taken part in the 101st Airborne's invasion of Normandy. Now that I knew that he was just seventeen years old at the time, his courage in the face of the German commander, endangering himself for my sake, was even more astounding. I remembered that even in "the Hellhole," he had carried himself like a man and shown exemplary consideration for others.

Kessler was living in Pittsburgh, and Lozano had moved from California to El Paso, Texas. During the next eight years, I spoke with each of them, but we were never able to meet face to face. When I called Ed Lozano in 2006, his wife told me that Ed was too sick to speak with me; Alzheimer's disease had robbed him of his memory. In 2007, I tried to arrange a meeting with Ed Kessler, with my son, Dan, videotaping our discussion of our POW experiences. But it was not to be. Ed's son called me back and said that the meeting would be detrimental to his father's health: his troubled emotional baggage from the past could trigger a dangerous reaction.

I reflected on this phenomenon. Out of the four of us—Urda, Kessler, Lozano and me—I was the only one to live out my life free of long-term psychiatric results and had kept all of my mental faculties. True, I had suffered some trauma, but it was nothing compared to the endless hell my friends went through. I remembered my heartfelt prayers during those maddening three days in the cattle car: "Please, don't let me lose my sanity!" At the time, I gave thanks for the short-term answer to my plea. Could an earnest prayer have a lifelong effect?

While in Denver back in the summer of 1998, I had also called Greg and Helen Urda, Andy's son and widow. They were very enthusiastic about the finding of the *Barracuda* and said that they were planning to attend the 11th Armored Division convention in Kentucky that year. They urged me to come. I was a little reluctant, falling back on my own studied indifference to the war and its memories. I had only been to one such gathering, and that

The former ASTP students assigned to Company B, 41st Tank Battalion, developed a close friendship that is still going strong. Pictured here at the 11th Armored Division Reunion in 2005 (left to right) are Ted Hartman, Jules Levine, me, and Wayne Van Dyke.

was fifty-one years earlier. But June and I hadn't seen the Urdas in over twenty years, so we decided to take in the convention on our way back to Israel.

I was not sorry that I went to the reunion, for I met there another close friend, Wayne Van Dyke. I had not seen him since our first day in battle, fifty-four years before. The first sergeant of our company, Lynwood Ammonds, and his wife, Doris, were also there. What a nostalgic get-together that was, this time with our wives, pictures of our children, and five decades worth of stories to tell.

In the year 2000, two years after my first visit to Bastogne, Roger Marquet called again to invite me to another ceremony, this time commemorating fifty-five

After the tank ceremony (left to right): Ellen and Greg Urda, Alene Urda, Helen Urda, and June and Ivan Goldstein. My warm friendship with the Urda family has continued long beyond Andy's passing. In 2006, at the 11th Armored Association reunion, Greg brought his cello and asked me for a few moments of my time. We went into another room. "This is for you," he said softly, and then played his gift—a beautiful arrangement of the Israeli anthem, "Hatikvah."

years since the end of the war in Europe. In light of the history I had provided to them, a special plaque would be attached to the *Barracuda,* along with the insignia of the 11th Armored Division. The event would welcome veterans of the 11th and especially family members of the tank's crew. This time, I felt no hesitation. I told Roger that June and I would be honored and happy to attend.

We called Roger the night we got to Bastogne, and he said that he would meet us at the tank in the morning. Did

I detect a slight chuckle in his voice? After breakfast, as we walked toward the tank, another figure was crossing the square, and it wasn't Roger. As the man approached, to my great surprise and elation, I recognized the familiar face of my old friend, Ted Hartman. Another ASTP comrade, Ted was a tank driver in the 11th Armored. Fifty-six years had passed since our tanks were separated during that day in battle, and we had not seen each other since just after the war. After a warm embrace, he told me that he had picked up the dedication story on the Internet and came to Bastogne to surprise me. Over the next few days, we shared the stories of our lives and families. The *Barracuda* had reunited us. The Urdas and my ASTP foursome in Company B of the 41st Battalion, including Ted, Jules Levine, and Wayne Van Dyke, pledged to get together every year, for as long as we are able.

The plaque dedication ceremony at the tank pulled together a number of veterans and family members of the 11th Armored Division. Letters were read from family members of Alexander, Peterman, and Hebert. The square was filled with city and government officials and citizens from the area. Again, there were special ceremonies for three days, with huge crowds attending. Most important and personally moving to me was that Helen Urda and two of Andy's children, Greg and Alene, were there with us. How proud Andy would have been. He would have savored this day and appreciated the recognition bestowed upon us.

215

The pigsty where we were locked up after being captured.

After the tank program, a group of the participants and media personnel traveled up to the Lhoas farm and the field where the *Barracuda* was stopped, for a retelling of our story. My unanswered question from our trip two years earlier still nagged me: "Where was the small stable that we were taken to after being captured?" I broke away from the group and wandered away from the farmhouse. All of a sudden, I spied a small brick shed across the driveway. I had not noticed it the last time. I tried the

216

door, but it was locked. Could this be the little barn in which we were locked up that first night? I asked Roger to get the key to the door. The minute the door swung open, the memory of that night came rushing back to me. This was it! Mrs. Lhoas told me later that the small building had been a pigsty before the war, but it was now a tool shed. The mystery was solved. All my recollections were now confirmed in hard brick.

The Pierlot family, grandchildren of Mr. Denis, who owned the meadow, invited us to their home and spent the evening with us and the Urda family. All the children and grandchildren, as well as other family members, had been gathered to meet us. With their son-in-law as interpreter, we discussed those harrowing war years and its impact on all of us. The family expressed, over and over, their eternal gratitude to the Americans for their liberation from the Nazis. Once again, they treated me like the American ambassador.

Epilogue

Looking Back, Looking Forward

IBEGAN MY STORY WITH what started as a beautiful day in Denver, December 7, 1941, a date that is indelibly engraved in the memory of every American who lived during that time. Our lives and our memories are filled with landmarks in time: personal, family, national, and religious dates. I now conclude my book with three special dates that occur in a one-week period.

Today, as I write my final chapter, it is a gorgeous day in Jerusalem. The date is May 2, 2008. Outside, it is quiet. The time is approaching 10:00 a.m. The silence is broken by the wail of a siren, sending out a piercing cry throughout the entire country of Israel. Every child and adult stops what he or she is doing and stands erect in silence. I am looking out from my balcony window toward the Knesset, the main street below, and the park across the street.

Vehicles have stopped moving; drivers and occupants stand beside them. Pedestrians on the street and people in the park are standing motionless as the siren continues. The day is Yom Hashoa, Holocaust Remembrance Day, the day designated to remember and pay homage to the six million Jewish victims who perished through Nazi barbarism during one of the blackest periods in mankind's history. For twenty-four hours, all forms of entertainment stop. Television programs shut down, except for news and programs related to the Holocaust. This type of memorial is unique in the whole world and recalls the history of persecution and slaughter that our nation has endured since its very beginnings.

The second of the three days is May 7, Yom Hazikaron, Remembrance Day. We remember and honor the soldiers and citizens who have lost their lives in the constant wars waged in the sixty years since Israel became a state. On the night of May 7 and through the next day, we will change our somber mood to one of great joy, celebration, and gratitude. Israel will celebrate the Jewish people's return to its homeland after two thousand years, and the establishment of a sovereign Jewish state—Yom Haatzmaut, Independence Day.

It is very significant to me that in 2008 the Hebrew date of Israel's Independence Day falls on the Gregorian calendar date of May 8. This is V-E Day, the anniversary of the end of World War II in Europe, the date that Nazi Germany was defeated sixty-three years ago.

The establishment of the State of Israel is inextricably tied to the ashes and the souls of six million victims and the many survivors of the Holocaust. During the sixty years since Israel's establishment, its enemies have initiated fierce wars aimed at Israel's destruction. Despite this ongoing attack by its Arab neighbors, this little democracy has developed into a veritable paradise. Israel has been in the forefront of the world's technological research in electronics, medicine, agriculture, and other fields, as well as excelling in the arts. This amazing country with its tiny piece of land has one of the world's greatest armies.

In two months, with God's help, June and I, together with our children, grandchildren, and great-grandchildren, will celebrate our sixtieth wedding anniversary, along with Israel's sixtieth anniversary. As I look back on my life, I am forever thankful to my mother's Partner for a life of deliverance, good health, success, children, grandchildren, great grandchildren, and the most wonderful wife imaginable. These are my greatest blessings. As I look toward the future, I hope and pray that God's countenance will shine upon us and guide us to a time when man will learn to live in peace.

Appendix
Family Lore

MY GREAT-GRANDPARENTS on my mother's maternal side, Moshe Yitzchak and Fega Goodstein, came from London to America with six young children around the year 1870. They traveled across America in a covered wagon, settling in Denver, Colorado. This was before Colorado became a state.

My grandmother Taube Esther was the third of the Goodstein's six young children. My grandfather, my mother's father, Abraham Greinetz, was born in Brest-Litovsk, a town on the Russian-Polish border. The name Greinetz means border. He set off from Brest-Litovsk to America by himself as a young teenager (probably to avoid serving in the Russian army). The date was in the late 1870s or early 1880s. He arrived in Denver, contacting relatives that left Brest-Litovsk before him. They changed their name from Greinetz to Grimes. The Goodstein and Greinetz families were among the earliest Jewish settlers in Colorado.

Abraham Greinetz and Taube Esther Goodstein were married in the late 1880s. This union produced eight children. Three of the children died at early ages. My mother, Ida Greinetz, was born in the year 1894, the third child of eight. My father, Max Goldstein, was the oldest of six children, born on the Lower East Side of New York to Zelig and Leah Goldstein, who came from the Polish-Russian area of Europe, via Ireland, to New York.

Max was born February 22, 1890. He was a blonde, blue-eyed, pug-nosed kid who took on the moniker "Murph," a name that stuck with him the rest of his life. He loved the entertainment professions and theater life of New York. He made many friends and acquaintances among the actors and entertainers around the stage-door areas of the city.

One of his idols was Pat Rooney, the great soft-shoe tap dancer, whose routines he learned and imitated to perfection. Although he never took lessons, he learned to play the piano and harmonica by ear. One of his friends, who became a confidante, was the great actress Marie Dressler. Murph learned the diamond-setting trade, a career that he excelled in. On a trip to Denver from New York to visit an aunt, he met Ida Greinetz on a blind date. It was love at first sight for Murph. They were married in 1920 after a whirlwind romance and courtship.

According to my mother, it was one of the great love affairs, even though it was tragically cut short by Murph's sudden and untimely death in 1930. Before the wedding,

Ida took a trip to Brooklyn to meet the Goldstein family. A strong bond and love quickly developed from the time of this initial meeting between Ida and the entire Goldstein family. The same bond and love existed between Ida's family and Murph.

Murph had taken a job with H. H. Clark Jewelers as a diamond setter but had the dream to open his own high-class jewelry store. He realized this dream a couple of years later, in 1922, with Murph and Ida working side by side at Murph's Jewelry and Gift Shop.

Bibliography

Degive, Jacques, Robert Fergloute, and Roger Marquet. *The "Sherman" at McAuliffe Square in Bastogne: The True Story*. Bastogne, Belgium: Cercle d'Histoire de Bastogne, 1999.

Hartman, J. Ted. *Tank Driver: With the 11th Armored from the Battle of the Bulge to VE Day*. Bloomington, Indiana: Indiana University Press, 2003.